T0360867

Emergency Services Management

An expert guide to contemporary research in the field of emergency services management, this short-form book will help academics, scholars, and practitioners to appreciate the important role and contribution of these services.

Contemporary emergency services have been rapidly changing in response to increasing demand, reducing resources, the impact of COVID-19 and the increasingly complex threats to public safety. Academics, practitioners, the emergency services and their key stakeholders all need to have a clear understanding of the changing role and contribution of these services as well as finding ways to improve their management and performance so that policy solutions to new and emerging threats may be efficiently developed and effectively implemented. The book looks at the application of public management theories to emergency services and the development of professionalism within the police, fire and rescue, and ambulance services. It examines the increasing need for better collaboration and identifies the nature and extent of the academic and practitioner divide and the research gap between the academic and professional communities in each of the services.

This book will be invaluable to researchers, scholars, practitioners, and students in the fields of governance, leadership, and management, especially those focusing on emergency services and management during crises.

Paresh Wankhade is Professor of Leadership and Management at Edge Hill University, Lancashire, UK.

Peter Murphy is a Professor of Public Policy and Management at Nottingham Trent University, UK.

State of the Art in Business Research
Series Editor: Geoffrey Wood

Recent advances in theory, methods and applied knowledge (alongside structural changes in the global economic ecosystem) have presented researchers with challenges in seeking to stay abreast of their fields and navigate new scholarly terrains.

State of the Art in Business Research presents shortform books which provide an expert map to guide readers through new and rapidly evolving areas of research. Each title will provide an overview of the area, a guide to the key literature and theories and time-saving summaries of how theory interacts with practice.

As a collection, these books provide a library of theoretical and conceptual insights, and exposure to novel research tools and applied knowledge, that aid and facilitate in defining the state of the art, as a foundation stone for a new generation of research.

Comparative Corporate Governance
A Research Overview
Thomas Clarke

Brands and Consumers
A Research Overview
Jaywant Singh and Benedetta Crisafulli

Emergency Services Management
A Research Overview
Paresh Wankhade and Peter Murphy

For more information about this series, please visit: www.routledge.com/State-of-the-Art-in-Business-Research/book-series/START

Emergency Services Management

A Research Overview

Paresh Wankhade and Peter Murphy

LONDON AND NEW YORK

First published 2023
by Routledge
4 Park Square, Milton Park, Abingdon, Oxon OX14 4RN

and by Routledge
605 Third Avenue, New York, NY 10158

Routledge is an imprint of the Taylor & Francis Group, an informa business

British Library Cataloguing-in-Publication Data
A catalogue record for this book is available from the British Library

ISBN: 978-1-032-05543-5 (hbk)
ISBN: 978-1-032-05544-2 (pbk)
ISBN: 978-1-003-19801-7 (ebk)

DOI: 10.4324/9781003198017

Typeset in Times New Roman
by Apex CoVantage, LLC

Contents

Preface

Emergency services operation is a global provision, but their management and organisational understanding is beginning to open a clear theory-practice divide in the current research landscape. This short volume endeavours to demystify some of the key issues in the emergency services organisations and to examine this theory-practice divide.

Scholarly understanding of emergency services is hampered by complex legislative and political landscape, different management structures, numerous funding models, and commissioning frameworks with little to compare between them. This has also recently been accompanied by an unprecedented period of change brought about by a global climate of fiscal austerity, changing socio-economic conditions, growing numbers of natural disasters, and pandemics and new forms of security threats to mention a few. Notwithstanding these challenges, these organisations have made significant progress in upskilling the workforce, adopting new technology and the application of mainstream management tools to improve performance and service delivery. The study of emergency organisations can potentially offer great insights into organisational resilience, interoperability, collaboration, and leadership behaviours.

One of the key aims of the book is to make sense of the quite heterogeneous body of existing literature in order to extend the debate and consolidate the knowledge base paying particular attention to authoritative sources published in leading scholarly outlets. The impact of the COVID-19 pandemic on the emergency services has been profound both on organisational delivery and organisational resilience and on staff health and wellbeing. We have, however, had to be selective in choosing the themes for investigation due to the format of this series and consciously didn't dwell on the workforce issues having recently written extensively elsewhere. Our key objective has been to provide readers with a critical perspective on the state of business research within the neglected settings of emergency service organisations which is the commendable aim of the State of Art in Business series. We sincerely hope that we have done justice to our brief.

Emergency service organisations have much to offer to management and organisation studies scholars because of their global manifestation and their adoption of management tools and new hybrid forms of governance structures. Our analysis suggests that the 'research-practice gap' can only be addressed by a significant collaborative effort between academics, professionals, and practitioners with an active bridging role played by governments, policy makers, staff associations, professional bodies, think tanks and other potential boundary spanners.

January 2023
Paresh Wankhade
Peter Murphy

Acknowledgement

This book would not have been completed without the help and encouragement of many people to whom we would like to express our sincere gratitude. We would like to thank the Routledge *State of the Art in Business Research Series* Editor Professor Geoffrey Wood, our publisher Routledge Books, and in particular Terry Clague, Senior Publisher for their continuous support, encouragement and patience in completing this project.

We would have not completed this work without the support and understanding of our respective families (Kavita, Gaurav, and Divij; Stephanie and Robert) to write up this book.

This book is an important contribution to the Series in exploring the state of research in emergency services which are relatively neglected by the management and organisational studies scholars. Important insights can be gained about the practice of leadership, organisational resilience, and interoperability in both emotionally challenging and dynamic environments and their more routine or everyday organisational settings. We sincerely hope that this volume will rekindle further research interest about the nature and working of emergency organisations and will help attract a new breed of academics, professionals, and practitioners in the quest for theory building and carrying out empirical research in difficult and extreme settings.

Paresh Wankhade
Peter Murphy

1 Emergency services management

A research overview

Introduction and background

The purpose of this book is to present an overview of contemporary research in the field of emergency services management. It is about research into the business and management of the emergency services and in particular, the three services that are colloquially known as the 'blue light' services namely the police, ambulance, and fire and rescue services.

All three of the 'blue light' emergency services have changed significantly since the turn of the century, reflecting both the increased range and the changing nature of the risks that contemporary society and local communities now face, and the response from emergency services (Newton and Hodge, 2012; Wankhade et al., 2019; McCann and Granter, 2019; Wankhade and Patnaik, 2019; Murphy et al., 2020). This has led to changes to the organisations themselves and how they are governed and managed. For instance, Tony Blairs' New Labour government in the U.K. from 1997, famously tried to 'modernise' and facilitate the continuous improvement of all locally delivered public services including the three blue light services (Finlayson, 2003; Stewart, 2003; Savage, 2007; Department of Health, 2000; Murphy and Greenhalgh, 2018). It was not, however, in any way unique and much of this 'performance' agenda was reflected in similar agendas in North America, across Europe and in Australasia.

'Modernisation' and the turn of the century provide the logical starting point for a review of 'contemporary' business and management research. It also provides two contrasting periods, that is, the years before and after the Great Recession of 2007–2009. The first period generally saw increasing investment in public services, including the emergency services, while the second period generally experienced continuous and significant reductions in financial support for emergency services up to the outbreak of the COVID-19 pandemic. (Marmot et al., 2010, 2020; National Audit Office (NAO), 2011, 2015a, 2015b; Murphy and Greenhalgh, 2018; HM Treasury, 2021).

DOI: 10.4324/9781003198017-1

Despite subsequent social, economic, environmental, and political changes, the need to facilitate continuous improvement and the obligation to achieve Best Value and Value for Money have remained as statutory obligations and fundamental objectives of the services in the U.K. since they were introduced by New Labour at the turn of the century. This also resonated with the new public management (NPM) agenda across the OECD countries and the growing popularity of some of the instruments highlighted earlier.

Academics, practitioners, and the emergency services' key stakeholders need to have a clear understanding of the changing role and contribution of these services as well as finding ways to improve their management and performance so that policy solutions to new and emerging threats may be efficiently developed and effectively implemented. In the recent past, a systematic and collective understanding of the challenges and opportunities facing the services has been hampered by a significant divide between theory and practice and the dominance of professional literature at the cost of balanced inquiry (Wankhade and Murphy, 2012). Academia needs to be relevant to practice and practice needs the legitimation of being theoretically robust. It is therefore in the public interest for each to engage with the other. The divide may be different in each of the three services although in all three cases the nature of the divide has recently changed as the emergency services have sought to develop and professionalise their management and staff and academics have increasingly been encouraged to demonstrate the social and economic impacts of their work in wider society and not just their contribution to scholarship and academic endeavour (see Wankhade et al., 2019; Murphy et al., 2020; McCann and Granter, 2019).

The strategic and operational challenges of delivering a safe and adequate level of service in the context of severe budgetary cuts, political pressures, and external 'shocks' such as the U.K.'s withdrawal from the EU, the climate crises, the global COVID-19 pandemic, and the direct and indirect social, economic, and environmental impacts of the war in Ukraine have compelled organisations to re-focus on the principles of economy, efficiency, and effectiveness of their service delivery while experimenting (and challenging) notions of 'leadership', 'accountability', risk management', 'innovation', 'culture', 'professionalism', 'wellbeing', 'resilience', and 'sustainability'.

While there is a growing body of literatures about these concepts, they have emerged in parallel to the new and more practical publications emanating from emergency services learning and training. With the advent of a post-COVID-19 landscape and in anticipation of further reductions in financial support, this appears to be an appropriate time to take stock, review contemporary research, and provide a fresh perspective. The impact of COVID-19 pandemic on the emergency services has been profound, both on organisational delivery and resilience and on staff health and wellbeing

(Tehrani, 2022; Dai et al., 2021; Pink et al., 2021; Heath et al., 2021; HMIC-FRS, 2021a, 2021b; Wankhade, 2021).

Emergency services management remains an under-researched field. Our aim is to present an empirical overview of the development of knowledge in the field and to suggest some areas for future investment. This book is as much concerned with the advancement of the 'theory' of emergency management as it is with analysing the implications for professionals in the field. It is not intended to bridge the various divides, but it is attempting to narrow a gap in the knowledge and understanding of both sides.

The next section will examine the theoretical antecedents of different public management theories and their application to emergency services. Later in the book, we will look in more detail at the theory-practice divide as it has developed and changed in the three blue light services and address the question of whether there is a single divide or whether there are actually three different divides.

Theoretical antecedents

Practice-based research, practice-led research, and practitioner research have all contributed to a strong theme in emergency services research since the 18th century when the traditional or classic model of 'top-down command and control' transferred from military campaigns and facilitated the industrial revolution. It was later to influence Weber in the development of the principles of bureaucracy theory and bureaucracy management theory, and later Henri Fayol, Frederick Taylor, and Woodrow Wilson as they conceptualised the origins of traditional western public administration.

The emergence of all three blue light emergency services was dominated by people who were primarily practitioners. In 1829, Sir Robert Peel the U.K. Home Secretary established a full-time, professional, and centrally organised police force for the Greater London area, the Metropolitan Police, based on ethical policing principals which are often used as the definition of policing by consent (Home Office, 2021). The nine 'Peelian' principals, which were probably devised by the first two Commissioners of Police of the Metropolis (Charles Rowan and Richard Mayne), still influence both the theory and practice of policing, originated from the instructions given to all new police officers in the Metropolitan Police (Reith, 1948, 1956; Grieve, 2015).

Edinburgh's Great Fire of 1824 led to James Braidwood institutionalising the principles of effective firefighting and leading the establishment of fire services in Edinburgh, and later in London (Ewen, 2010). Braidwood himself wrote three seminal publications, one of which was an article in the *Journal of the Royal Society of Arts*, which influenced firefighting internationally during the industrial revolutions, but which still resonate through contemporary services (Braidwood, 1830, 1856, 1866; Ewen, 2010).

It was from the experience of wars and the existence of field hospitals that ambulance services developed. Dr. Dominique Jean Larrey, a surgeon in Bonaparte's Napoleonic wars, is credited with developing lightweight horse drawn wagons to transport the wounded to field hospitals and bring aid to people in battle, which became known as 'flying ambulances' because of their speed (Arndt, 2018; Pollock, 2013). In America the U.S. Civil war from 1861 prompted the establishment of the first U.S. Army Ambulance Corp in 1862 and Liverpool established the first U.K. service in 1883.

Traditional public administration (TPA) theory also had its roots in the mid-1800s, where advanced western countries used its concepts and approaches to standardise their financial and banking systems, with a view to improving business operations at management levels among private and public organisations (Hood, 1991; Entwistle, 2022). The theoretical foundations of TPA are ostensibly derived from Max Weber in Germany, Woodrow Wilson and Frederick Taylor in the U.S., and the Northcote–Trevelyan Report of 1854 about the Civil Service in the U.K.

The top-down command and control model transferred from the military to the British Civil Service which, being based on a hierarchical model, led Weber to identify and develop the principles of 'modern' bureaucracy (bureaucracy theory or bureaucratic management theory). For Weber, bureaucracy involves a hierarchical system, that is, a system of control in which policy is set at the top and carried out through a series of offices, with each manager and worker or a group of workers reporting to a superior and held to account by that person. Ultimately the role of the bureaucrat is subordinate to the political superior.

Woodrow Wilson differentiated public administration from political decision making and thought the administration of policy should be underpinned by a set of principles. Administrators should be non-partisan, should serve all citizens (the public interest), and be held to high standards. Well-educated, but neutral they should advance on merit rather than through political appointment or patronage. Public administration was not business, but it should be carried out in a business-like manner and learn from business. F.W. Taylor was a pioneer for industrial efficiency and the productivity of labour and his seminal book *The Principles of Scientific Management* (1911) promoted the pursuit of efficiency in public bureaucracy and the use of empirical evidence in both theory and practice.

As mentioned earlier, bureaucratic theories and principles provided the bedrock to the development of public administration that dominated theory and practice for a large part of the 20th century at both national and local administrative levels. In the 19th century, the development of public services (such as utilities, water, and energy provision) was originally provided at the local community level before being 'nationalised'. Weber and Wilson, however, encouraged a principle-agent form of accountability (Entwistle, 2022). In the U.K. and Europe their development also coincided with the early development and expansion of the three blue light services, particularly after they emerged from the second world war when a large number of ex-servicemen joined all three services and significantly influenced their operating environment and organisational cultures. Bayley (1992) compares the organisation of policing in Australia, Canada, Great Britain, India, and the U.S., while in the same book Reiss (1992) describes the 20th-century evolution of policing in the U.S.

In the U.K., as in many countries during the second half the century, all three services were reviewed and overhauled and most significantly restructured and transferred to local administrative control. Although oversight and policy remained with central government departments both the Police and Fire Services became the responsibility of County Councils and County Boroughs, while the Ambulance service became part of the NHS, albeit operationally run by local authorities (Caple, 2004; Pollock, 2015; Arndt, 2018). The question then arose about how much autonomy or local control should the delivery agent be allowed or empowered with? Entwistle (2022: 2) argues, 'In real terms then autonomy reforms promise . . . . a degree of *freedom from* something (like political interference or central government bureaucracy) with a view the *freedom to* focus on something else (like a particular policy problem or the needs of the client)'.

Entwistle also quotes Rainey and Steinbauer's enthusiasm for autonomy as a key driver for public service effectiveness but even they acknowledge that absolute authority isn't feasible (Hood, 1976). As Rainey and Steinbauer (1999: 16) pointed out, 'Government agencies will be more effective when they have higher levels of autonomy in relation to external stakeholders but not extremely high levels of autonomy'.

During this period both theory and practice together with policy and delivery of the blue light services, was strongly associated with local control and the traditional notions of public administration research. The next section analyses the nature and the variability of the research-practice gap in each of the three emergency services.

The second half of the 20th century was also notable for three things:

• Theoretical plurality as new management theories emerged;
• Different levels of interest in the three services from academic researchers;
• Institutional stability in the three services and in their relationship to national government.

This period saw the rapid development of 'political science' as a discipline in its own right and increasing reference to public management rather than public administration. Managerialism and Institutionalism, the approach to the study of politics that focuses on formal institutions of government, both developed. The management concepts of Fayol and F.W. Taylor developed into managerialism, and for some academic authors managerialism became a full-fledged ideology. Managerialism emphasised the value of *professional managers* and the concepts and methods they use. Managerialism in the public sector promoted the idea that public institutions and organisations should be run 'as if' these were for-profit entities. They should become not just 'business like'—but they should be businesses and duplicate private sector business systems and processes together with their values and norms. The predominant definition of neo-liberalism makes the underlying assumption that business operations are more efficient and effective in the private sector than the public sector (now a demonstrably false and flawed assumption). However, for the last 50 years this assumption has strongly influenced policy formulation in the U.S., the U.K., Europe Australia, and other advanced nations (Hayek, 1944; Friedman and Schwartz, 1963; Quiggin, 1999; Navarro, 2007; Muzio and Kirkpatrick, 2011; Muzio et al., 2013).

Classical economists distinguish between:

- Exchange value (i.e. price of something on an open market).
- Labour value (amount of human effort invested in items of production).
- Use value (how useful something is to a person or situation).

The neo-liberal economic approaches have focused on measuring exchange value at the expense of both labour value and use value. Neo-liberalism became a set of policy prescriptions that endorses a free-market ideology to facilitate business operations towards achieving organisational goals. The main aim of neo-liberalism was to encourage competition among organisations which would enhance economic efficiency. It also seeks to reduce welfare activities while encouraging markets to function more freely. With the move to local service delivery and particularly after the public service reforms of the 1970's and 80's agency theory began to be adopted by public management scholars seeing, for example, local authorities as local deliverers of public services and 'agents' of central government. An agent is employed by a principal to undertake activity on the principals' behalf—obvious examples are when governments ask local authorities to deliver services according to government policies and priorities or when public officials act as agents for politicians. Agency theory maintains that the objectives of agents is often different from those of their principals but may be left unmonitored and uncontrolled. This may result in agents not meeting the satisfaction of the principals. Hence, one central aim of agency theory is to enable principals to control and monitor the behaviours of the agents so as to avoid paying higher agency costs.

The development of institutionalism in public management was greatly influenced by the emerging political science view of institutionalism, that is, methodological approaches in political science that have at their core an emphasis on institutions, understood as the rules, regularities, structures, and the context more generally which influence political outcomes and shape political conduct.

In Weber's *The Protestant Ethic and the Spirit of Capitalism* (1904) Weber had developed the concept of the 'iron cage of bureaucracy' which is said to trap individuals in systems based purely on efficiency, rational calculation, and control. Lammers and Garcia (2017: 1) state that

> Institutional theory (generally) seeks to explain organizational communication in terms of shared pre-existing rules, beliefs, and norms in the external environment of organizations. While its sociological origins rest on the concepts of legitimacy, rational myths, and isomorphic forces in organizational fields, communicative institutionalism emphasizes forms of discourse, such as rhetoric, framing, messages, vocabularies, tropes, narratives, slogans, metaphors, idioms, and selective grammatical styles to show how communication has the force to alter cognition and thus social institutions.

Public Choice Theory developed as the application of economic tools to deal with traditional problems previously more associated with political science, that is, when a service or good is not already amenable to deployment, distribution, or development by an existing market Public Choice Theory therefore applies economics to the study of traditional public administration issues and generates quasi-markets, privatisation, and contracting out to foster competition (Buchanan and Tollison, 1984; Mashaw, 1997; Boyne, 1998; Dunleavy, 1991).

NPM developed in the U.S. and the U.K. in the 1970s and 1980s at the same time as monetary policy increasingly supplanted fiscal policy as the main economic policy designed to bring stability to gross domestic product, to achieve and maintain low unemployment, and to maintain predictable exchange rates with other currencies (Barzelay, 1993; Pollitt and Bouckaert, 2011, 2017). Ronald Reagan and Margaret Thatcher were greatly attracted to neoliberalism and monetary policy, and the 20th century resurgence of ideas associated with free-market capitalism. They believed in increased market competition, dismantling of state monopolies, the transfer of state assets to private individuals, and the reduction of public bureaucracies and so-called red tape. NPM developed in public management partly as a response to the perceived or alleged inflexibility of Traditional Public Administration and became associated with the slogan of 'let managers manage'.

Governments faced internal and external economic and financial shocks and challenges such as globalisation, climate change, and the energy market. The growth of neo-liberal market economics from the early 1980s, increasingly focused debate and policy onto the cost and size of government and the perceived need for growth and innovation in the private sector. This led governments to engage in a range of policies (now grouped under NPM) to review organisational structures and management styles in a more effective and cost-efficient public sector to achieve better outcomes, including quality service delivery and value for money (Entwistle, 2022; Noordegraaf, 2015; Samaratunge and Bennington, 2002).

To an extent NPM was really a case of a theoretical paradigm as 'ex-post facto rationalising practice' as Hood noted the adoption and emerging dominance of NPM across developed and some developing nations worldwide which he saw as one of the 'most intriguing' trends in public administration (1991: 3). Osborne and Gaebler (1992) argued (or perhaps over-idealised it as) a shift from an over-bureaucratic inflexible system to a more flexible administration with key principles such as steering rather than rowing, empowering rather than serving, earning rather than spending, funding outcomes rather than inputs, transforming rule-driven organisations, meeting customer needs rather than wants and teamwork participation rather than hierarchical participation. However, one key impact NPM had on public management was that governments were increasingly confined to facilitating, leading, and catalysing changes to achieve greater outputs with limited financial resources and fewer personnel. Efficiency rather than effectiveness, short-term and individual targets and outputs rather than long-term or collective goals and aspirations, with little attention to inherent values or the public interest and the relegation of social and environmental concerns to economic performance.

In emergency services, the very existence of which had always been legitimised as being in the 'public interest' and predominantly evaluated on a collective or population basis, the application of NPM and its conceptualisations, were clearly challenging and contested (Pollitt, 1995; McCann and Granter, 2019). The gap between policy, theory, and practice inevitably widened. Despite numerous attempts and successive governments enthusiasm for 'privatisation' and 'marketisation' the majority of police, fire, and ambulance services remained within the public domain operated in the interest of the public and creating public or social value rather than merely individual value. Although both reforms and research based upon NPM theories and mechanisms were attempted this had only limited impact in the emergency services and often resulted in perverse outcomes and/or unintended consequences (Wankhade and Patnaik, 2019; Murphy et al., 2020).

One gap or three—the experience of the individual blue light services

Against this background of theoretical pluralism, the effectiveness and relevance of academic research to practice started to vary between fields and disciplines. We will examine the research-practice gap in detail in Chapter 5. However, ambulance and paramedic services, perhaps inevitably, gradually became drawn to the 'evidence-based practice' tradition, that is particularly strong in public health, nursing and the NHS more generally. This tradition uses the best available research evidence to inform and underpin nursing practice, policy, and education (Tucker and Leach, 2017). However, while advances (albeit modest) were made in health and safety and clinical practice within ambulance services, there was very little research devoted to the leadership and management of the ambulance service and the conveyance of patients to and from hospital (Granter et al., 2019; Wankhade and Mackway-Jones, 2015; Newton and Hodge, 2012; McCann et al., 2013; NAO, 2011; Snooks et al., 2009; Department of Health, 2005). Major change and restructuring in the development and governance of the NHS generated considerable empirical and non-empirical research adopting a variety of theoretical perspectives from traditional public administration, managerialism, and institutionalism but the service itself attracted little academic research in this period which was in stark contrast to the other parts of the NHS and to healthcare more generally (Wankhade et al., 2020, 2018).

Fire and rescue services were similar in the sense that they had a strong adherence to evidence-based policy and decision-making and robust justification for changes in standards and practice (Ewen, 2010; Murphy and Greenhalgh, 2018), which had led to a plethora of trade and professional journals and periodicals but little in academic journals with even fewer attempts to theorise the models and behaviours. There were areas that academics proliferated, such as in fire engineering, resistant materials, the psychology of trauma and others but in management terms (unlike the NHS) there was only one major restructuring of fire and rescue services in the second half of the 20th century and that was as part of the local government structural and financial re-organisations in the 1970s. The one managerial area that stands out was in human resource management and industrial relations research and even this was limited as relatively stable industrial relations were achieved by consultation and negotiation between fire and rescue authorities as employers and recognised trade unions through national negotiating arrangements. The other characteristic that they shared with ambulance services but contrasted strongly with the experience of the police is that they attracted little public and media interest and scored much higher on customer and public satisfaction polling. Fire and rescue services were strongly associated with the public interest and what little management research was generated tended to follow the same theoretical perspectives from traditional public administration, managerialism, and institutionalism.

The police services and their relationship with the law and the Criminal Justice System have, however, continued to excite both academic and practitioner interest throughout the late 20 century. The academic journal listings and their ratings for business and management show the number and variety of management perspectives on policing, generating a significant increase in empirical and non-empirical research. Policing is also clearly of interest to a much wider variety of academic disciplines and fields than either fire services or the ambulance services with law, sociology, psychology, politics, economics, history, human geographers, and others all investigating from their various perspectives, while inevitably interdisciplinary research also became more common.

While NPM has been the dominant paradigm in management it has never completely been accepted by public management scholars or by emergency service scholars. Direct delivery by public organisations rather than contracting or hybridisation remains the predominant form of service delivery. The emergence of public (and social) value within new public governance and new public service theories reinstates public interest, public values, and the creation of public value as the focus of research and discourse. The new public service approach (Denhardt and Denhardt, 2002, 2015) is rooted in democratic principles and active public participation. Governments serve rather than indirectly representing citizens as in democratic theory, it emphasises the accountability of officials to citizens, whereby officials serve and respond to citizens rather than steering society. Officials serving the ancient Greek concept of the *demos* rather than steering the *demos* as politicians might prefer.

The more recent concept of public value was originally developed from the works of Moore (1995) and Bozeman (2002) but has generated a new discourse and an alternative perspective for theorising public services that has now been developed more widely in North America, the U.K., Europe, Australia, and New Zealand (O'Flynn, 2007; Meynhardt, 2009; Benington and Moore, 2011; Bryson et al., 2015; Lindgreen et al., 2019; Wylie, 2020; Mazzucato, 2013, 2021). Moore's publications straddle three fields namely public management, criminal justice, and social innovation, which are coincidentally three areas very poorly served by NPM

Liddle (2021) helpfully defines new public governance as:

> a new paradigm including a set of doctrines and approaches aimed at promoting 'common good' by incorporating 'public values' across

the political system. It attempts to theorize about complex 'decision making' spaces and enlarged 'gaps' between formalized, hierarchical 'tiers' of regulatory government jurisdictions and informal, unregulated connections, linkages, and inter-relationships. The paradigm facilitates an understanding of inter-connections, inter-dependencies, interactions between complex issues and across multiple boundaries, to reach agreement between diverse stakeholders influencing what constitutes 'public value'.

(Liddle, 2021: 1)

The common factor with the new public service and new public governance discourses are the centrality of empirically based research, and a desire to close both the theory-practice divide and the contemporary policy and practice divide. This makes them an attractive perspective for emergency services research. Although there was an operational focus to Moore's earliest work this has been expanded to embrace values, behaviour, mental health, and wellbeing (Meynhardt, 2009; Lindgreen et al., 2019), while demonstrating how the creation of public value can be evaluated (Kelly et al., 2002; Mulgan, 2011; Moore, 2013; Dhanani and Thomas, 2019; Mulgan et al., 2019; Heath et al., 2021).

The structure of the book

There has been a strong desire across all three services for their core operational workforce to be considered as professionals and the service to be treated as a profession as a means of protecting their interests, promoting their influence, and ultimately encouraging recruitment to the services. The next chapter therefore investigates the state of professionalisation in the three services and explores whether the traditional 'traits' of a profession are either extant or in development.

Chapter 3 will then explore the state of collaborative activity across the services. Collaboration is increasingly considered a fundamental aspect of delivering emergency services. The challenging fiscal climate and the continuing demand to maximise efficiencies and reduce costs, is also generating repeated calls for a more collaborative or even integrationist approach to emergency management despite recent experience with major incidents suggesting it is far from being a panacea. We also discuss conceptual and methodological challenges including the barriers to effective collaboration.

Another prominent and ubiquitous theme of management inquiry is the demand for better and more effective leadership. Good leaders and effective leadership are essential for a healthy organisational culture and continuously improving services. Historically, emergency services have been organisationally structured in a hierarchical manner with clear command and control lines of communication to support ranks and seniority. In Chapter 4, we look at the current leadership structures and styles within the emergency services, followed by a brief look at the organisational culture of emergency services.

In Chapter 5, we return to the research-practice gaps in emergency services to look in more detail at the nature and scale of these gaps and whether there are opportunities to reduce or close the divisions. To do this, we adopt and adapt a conceptual framework from public management accounting which differentiates research producers or providers from research users or potential commissioners with a community of potential boundary spanners or bridging agencies that can potentially influence both communities (Dudau et al., 2015; Ferry et al., 2019). We then apply the model to each of the three services and identify some current challenges.

Finally in Chapter 6 we summarise our views, draw some brief conclusions and suggest that despite the challenging context, emergency services research is ripe for greater collaboration between academics, professionals, and practitioners. Allowing the research-practice gap to grow is in no one's interest and we would reiterate that academics and academia needs to be relevant to practice and practice needs the legitimacy and support of being theoretically robust.

Conclusion

This chapter has sought to contribute to the understanding and advancement of the 'theory' of emergency management and its application to the three emergency services. In the emergency services, traditional bureaucratic features such as hierarchy and command and control have never completely disappeared. If they exist 'below the surface' in other parts of public management, they are clearly still visible above the surface in many parts of the emergency services. Entwistle suggests that public management research is also neo-bureaucratic in the sense that other principles of bureaucracy such as formalisation, merit, and officers' neutrality have continued to develop 'in ways that have taken them some distance from the original understanding of those ideas' (Entwistle, 2022: 4). Neo-bureaucratic, institutional, and agency approaches therefore remain relatively healthy within emergency services research.

Governments have, of course, always relied on markets and marketisation to provide goods and services. However, the deliberate creation of new forms of quasi-markets (e.g., via purchaser-provider splits) and market-like conditions is a much more recent phenomenon. Governments also used freedoms and flexibility and the reduction of bureaucracy to encourage entrepreneurialism and innovation. NPM and managerialism with their emphasis on marketisation, outsourcing and allowing managers the freedom to manage, while undoubtedly widespread and heavily promoted, did not attain the level of hegemony in the provision of emergency services as it did in other parts of the public sector. Emergency services, in our view, have proved particularly resistant and inhospitable to NPM and public choice in both theory and practice notwithstanding the managerial and regulatory controls which are further restricting the autonomy of the work force (McCann and Granter, 2019; Corman, 2017; Noordegraaf, 2015).

New public governance's focus on collaboration, co-production, and partnership working was, however, much more acceptable and attractive to emergency services and resonated strongly with a lot of their experiences in practice. Networks, collaborations, and partnership working between the emergency services and with other public and non-profit agencies have become increasingly integral to the services as complex wicked issues, shared services co-production and multi-level government have gained prominence since the 1990s. This also revitalised the interest in stakeholder theory and stakeholder management was a building block for Mark Moore's original work on public value Moore (1995). Some, such as Liddle quoted earlier, see public value and its subsequent development as a paradigm within new public governance.

Comparative public administration (or management) such as Pollitt and Bouckaert's study of public management reforms across Europe, America, and Australia, demonstrates that the influence of different forms of social, economic, and institutional environments means that policies and initiatives that work in one country do not necessarily work as well in others.

We would suggest that practitioners reading this book would recognise some if not all, of the different theoretical positions from their practical experience and that rather than seeing public management theory as a single post-bureaucratic development. We agree with Entwistle (2022) and Thelen (2003) that they should be seen as overlapping and layered as elements of each are clearly discernible in emergency services research.

References

Arndt, C. (2018). *The History of the Ambulance Service*. Available at: the Emergency Services Information Portal at The History of the Ambulance Service— Emergency Services Ireland [Accessed 31 March 2022].

Barzelay, M. (1993). *The New Public Management*. New York: Russell Sage.

Bayley, D.H. (1992). Comparative organization of the police in English-speaking countries. In M. Tonry and N. Morris (eds.), *Modern Policing*, 509–545. Chicago: University of Chicago Press.

Benington, J., and Moore, M. (eds.). (2011). *Public Value Theory and Practice*. Basingstoke: Palgrave Macmillan.

Boyne, G. (1998). *Public Choice Theory and Local Government: A Comparative Analysis of the UK and the USA*. Basingstoke: Palgrave Macmillan.

Bozeman, B. (2002). Public-value failure: When efficient markets may not do. *Public Administration Review*, 62(2): 145–161.

Braidwood, J. (1830). *On the Construction of Fire-Engines and Apparatus, the Training of Firemen, and the Method of Proceeding in Cases of Fire*. Edinburgh: Oliver Boyd.

Braidwood, J. (1856). Fires: The best means of preventing and arresting them; with a few words on fire-proof structures. *Journal of the Royal Society of Arts*, IV(181): 413–460.

Braidwood, J. (1866). *Fire Prevention and Fire Extinction*. London: Bell and Daldry.

Bryson, J., Crosby, B., and Bloomberg, L. (eds.). (2015). *Creating Public Value in Practice Advancing the Common Good in a Multi-Sector, Shared-Power, No-One Wholly-in-Charge World*. Boca Raton: CRC Press.

Buchanan, J., and Tollison, R. (eds.). (1984). *The Theory of Public Choice-II*. Ann Arbor: University of Michigan.

Caple, L. (2004). *From Ambulances to Almonds*. Victoria: Trafford.

Corman, M.K. (2017). *Paramedics on and Off the Streets: Emergency Medical Services in the Age of Technological Governance*. Toronto: University of Toronto Press.

Dai, M., Xia, Y., and Han, R. (2021). The impact of lockdown on police service calls during the COVID-19 pandemic in China. *Policing: A Journal of Policy and Practice*, 15(3): 1867–1881.

Denhardt, J.V., and Denhardt, R.B. (2015). *The New Public Service*, 4th ed. Abingdon: Routledge.

Denhardt, R.B., and Denhardt, J.V. (2002). The new public service: Serving rather than steering. *Public Administration Review*, 60(6): 549–559.

Department of Health. (2000). *The NHS Plan: A Plan for Investment. A Plan for Reform*. London: HMSO.

Department of Health DH. (2005). *Taking Healthcare to the Patients: Transforming NHS Ambulance Services*. London: Department of Health.

Dhanani, A., and Thomas, G. (2019). Development NGOs and public value. In A. Lindgreen, N. Koenig-Lewis, M. Kitchiner, J. Brewer, M. Moore, and T. Meynhardt (eds.), *Public Value: Deepening, Enriching, and Broadening the Theory and Practice*. Abingdon: Routledge.

Dudau, A., Korac, S., and Saliterer, I. (2015). Mapping current engagement—Bridging the academic-practitioner gap. In *IRSPM SIG Accounting and Accountability*. Nottingham Trent University.

Dunleavy, P. (1991). *Democracy, Bureaucracy and Public Choice*. Brighton: Wheatsheaf.

Entwistle, T. (2022). *Public Management: A Research Overview*. Abingdon: Routledge Focus.

Ewen, S. (2010). *Fighting Fires: Creating the British Fire Service, 1800–1978*. Basingstoke: Palgrave Macmillan.

Ferry, L., Saliterer, I., Steccolini, I., and Tucker, B. (2019). *The Research-Practice Gap on Accounting in Public Services*. Cham, Switzerland: Springer.

Finlayson, A. (2003). *Making Sense of New Labour*. London: Lawrence & Wishart.

Friedman, M., and Schwartz, A. (1963). *A Monetary History of the United States.* Princeton, NJ: Princeton University Press.

Granter, E., Wankhade, P., McCann, L., Hassard, J., and Hyde, P. (2019). Multiple dimensions of work intensity: Ambulance work as edgework. *Work Employment and Society*, 33(2): 280–297.

Grieve, J. (2015). Historical perspective: British policing and the democratic ideal. Chapter 2 in P. Wankhade and D. Weir (eds.), *Police Services: Leadership and Management Perspectives*, 15–28. New York: Springer.

Hayek, F.A. (1944). *The Road to Serfdom.* Abingdon: Routledge.

Heath, G., Wankhade, P., and Murphy, P. (2021). Exploring the wellbeing of ambulance staff using the 'public value' perspective: opportunities and challenges for research. *Public Money and Management.* https://doi.org/10.1080/09540962.2021.1899613

HMICFRS. (2021a). *COVID-19 Inspection Letters.* Available at: https://www.justiceinspectorates.gov.uk/hmicfrs/search?sector=fire&cat=&frs=&year=&month=&s=%20Covid&type=publications [Accessed 18 November 2022].

HMICFRS. (2021b). *Responding to the Pandemic: The Fire and Rescue Service's Response to the COVID-19 Pandemic in 2020.* London: HMICFRS.

HM Treasury. (2021). *HMT Public Expenditure Statistical Analyses 2020 to 2020.* Available at: https://www.gov.uk/government/statistics/public-expenditure-statistical-analyses-2020 [Accessed 5 April 2022].

Home Office. (2021). *Definition of Policing by Consent.* FOI Release, 10 December 2021.

Hood, C. (1976). *The Limits of Administration.* London: John Wylie.

Hood, C. (1991). A public management for all seasons. *Public Administration*, 69(1): 3–19.

Kelly, G., Mulgan, G., and Muers, S. (2002). *Creating Public Value: An Analytical Framework for Public Service Reform.* London: Strategy Unit Cabinet Office.

Lammers, J.C., and Garcia, M.A. (2017). Institutional theory approaches. In C.R. Scott, J.R. Barker, T. Kuhn, J. Keyton, P.K. Turner, and L.K. Lewis (eds.), *The International Encyclopaedia of Organizational Communication*, 1–10. Hoboken, NJ: John Wiley & Sons, Ltd.

Liddle, J. (2021). New public governance. In R.A. List, H.K. Anheier, and S. Toepler (eds.), *International Encyclopaedia of Civil Society.* Cham: Springer. https://doi.org/10.1007/978-3-319-99675-2_9580-1

Lindgreen, A., Koenig-Lewis, N., Kitchener, M., Brewer, J., Moore, M., and Meynhardt, T. (2019). *Public Value: Deepening, Enriching, and Broadening the Theory and Practice.* Abingdon: Routledge.

Marmot, M., Allen, J., Boyce, T., Goldblatt, P., and Morrison, J. (2020). *Health Equity in England: The Marmot Review 10 Years On.* London: Institute of Health Equity.

Marmot, M., Allen, J., Goldblatt, P., Boyce, T., McNeish, D., Grady, D., and Geddes, I. (2010). *Fair Society Healthy Lives: Strategic Review of Health Inequalities in England Post-2010* (The Marmot Review). London: Institute of Health Equity.

Mashaw, J. (1997). *Greed, Chaos and Governance: Using Public Choice to Improve Public Law.* New Haven: Yale University Press.

Mazzucato, M. (2013). *The Entrepreneurial State: Debunking Public vs. Private Myths in Risk and Innovation*. London: Anthem Press.

Mazzucato, M. (2021). *Mission Economy: A Moonshot Guide to Changing Capitalism*. London: Allen Lane-Penguin.

McCann, L., and Granter, E. (2019). Beyond 'blue-collar professionalism': Continuity and change in the professionalization of uniformed emergency services work. *Journal of Professions and Organizations*, 6(3): 213–232.

McCann, L., Granter, E., Hyde, P., and Hassard, J. (2013). Still blue-collar after all these years? An ethnography of the professionalization of emergency ambulance work. *Journal of Management Studies*, 50: 750–776.

Meynhardt, T. (2009). Public value inside: What is public value creation? *International Journal of Public Administration*, 32(3): 192–219.

Moore, M. (1995). *Creating Public Value: Strategic Management in Government*. Cambridge, MA: Harvard University Press.

Moore, M. (2013). *Recognizing Public Value*. Cambridge, MA: Harvard University Press.

Mulgan, G. (2011). Effective supply and demand and the measurement of public and social value. In J. Bennington and M. Moore (eds.), *Public Value: Theory and Practice*. Basingstoke: Palgrave Macmillan.

Mulgan, G., Breckton, J., Tarrega, M., Bakhashi, H., Davies, J., Khan, H., and Finnis, A. (2019). *Public Value How Can It Be Measured, Managed and Grown?* Nesta Foundation. Available at: https://media.nesta.org.uk/documents/Public_Value_WEB.pdf [Accessed 4 April 2022].

Murphy, P., and Greenhalgh, K. (2018). The gathering storm: Modernisation, local alignment, and collaboration. Fire and rescue services under the early New Labour administration from 1997 to 2005. Chapter 2 in P. Murphy and K. Greenhalgh (eds.), *Fire and Rescue Services: Leadership and Management Perspectives*, 9–26. New York: Springer.

Murphy, P., Wankhade, P., and Lakoma, K. (2020). The strategic and operational landscape of emergency services in the UK. *International Journal of Emergency Services*, 9(1): 69–88.

Muzio, D., Brock, D.M., and Suddaby, R. (2013). Professions and institutional change: Towards an institutional sociology of the professions. *Journal of Management Studies*, 50: 699–721.

Muzio, D., and Kirkpatrick, I. (2011). Professions and organizations—a conceptual framework. *Current Sociology*, 59(4): 389–405.

National Audit Office. (2011). *Transforming NHS Ambulance Services*. London: TSO.

National Audit Office. (2015a). *Financial Sustainability of Police Forces in England and Wales*. HC 78, 2015–16. London: TSO.

National Audit Office. (2015b). *Financial Sustainability of Fire and Rescue Services*. HC 491, 2015–16. London: TSO.

Navarro, V. (2007). Neoliberalism as a class ideology; or the political causes of the growth of inequalities. *International Journal of Health Services*, 37(1): 47–62.

Newton, A., and Hodge, D. (2012). The ambulance service: The past, present and future. *Journal of Paramedic Practice*, 4(5): 303–305.

Noordegraaf, M. (2015). Hybrid professionalism and beyond. (New) forms of public professionalism in changing organizational and societal contexts. *Journal of Professions and Organizations*, 2(2): 187–206.

O'Flynn, J. (2007). From new public management to public value: Paradigmatic change and managerial implication. *Australian Journal of Public Administration*, 66(3): 353–366.

Osborne, D., and Gaebler, T. (1992). *Reinventing Government: How the Entrepreneurial Spirit Is Transforming the Public Sector*. New York: Plume Books.

Pink, J., Gray, N.S., O'Connor, C., Knowles, J.R., Simkiss, N.J., and Snowden, R.J. (2021). Psychological distress and resilience in first responders and health care workers during the COVID-19 pandemic. *Journal of Occupational and Organizational Psychology*, 94(4): 789–807.

Pollitt, C. (1995). 'Justification by works or by faith?'. 'Evaluating the new public management'. *Evaluation*, 12: 133–154.

Pollitt, C., and Bouckaert, G. (2011). *Public Management Reform: A Comparative Analysis—New Public Management, Governance, and the Neo-weberian State*, 3rd ed. Oxford: Oxford University Press.

Pollitt, C., and Bouckaert, G. (2017). *Public Management Reform: A Comparative Analysis—Into the Age of Austerity*. Oxford: Oxford University Press.

Pollock, A.C. (2013). Ambulance services in London and Great Britain from 1860 until today: A glimpse of history gleaned mainly from the pages of contemporary journals. *Emergency Medical Journal*, 30(3): 218–222.

Pollock, A.C. (2015). Historical perspectives in the ambulance service. Chapter 2 in P. Wankhade and K. Mackway-Jones (eds.), *Ambulance Services: Leadership and Management Perspectives*, 17–28. New York: Springer.

Quiggin, J. (1999). Globalisation, neoliberalism and inequality in Australia. *The Economic and Labour Relations Review*, 10(2): 240–259.

Rainey, H.G., and Steinbauer, P. (1999). Galloping elephants: Developing elements of a theory of effective government organisations. *Journal of Public Administration Research and Theory*, 9(1): 1–32.

Reiss, A.J. (1992). Police organization in the twentieth century. In M. Tonry and N. Morris (eds.), *Modern Policing*, 51–97. Chicago: University of Chicago Press.

Reith, C. (1948). *A Short History of the British Police*. Oxford: Oxford University Press.

Reith, C. (1956). *A New Study of Police History*. Edinburgh: Oliver Boyd.

Samaratunge, R., and Bennington, L. (2002). New public management: Challenge for Sri Lanka. *Asian Journal of Public Administration*, 24(1): 87–109.

Savage, S. (2007). *Police Reform Forces for Change*. Oxford: Oxford University Press.

Snooks, H., Evans, A., Wells, B., Peconi, J., Thomas, M., Woollard, M., Guly, H., Jenkinson, E., Turner, J., and Hartley-Sharpe, C. (2009). What are the highest priorities for research in emergency prehospital care? *Emergency Medicine Journal*, 26(2): 549–550.

Stewart, J. (2003). *Modernising British Local Government: An Assessment of Labour's Reform Programme*. Basingstoke: Palgrave Macmillan.

Taylor, F.W. (1911). *The Principles of Scientific Management*. New York: Harpers & Brothers.

Tehrani, N. (2022). The psychological impact of COVID-19 on police officers. *The Police Journal*, 95(1): 73–87.

Thelen, K. (2003). How institutions evolve: Insights from comparative-historical analysis. In J. Mahoney and D. Rueschemeyer (eds.), *Comparative Historical Analysis in the Social Sciences*, 208–240. Cambridge: Cambridge University Press.

Tucker, B., and Leach, M. (2017). Learning from the experience of others. Lessons on the research-practice gap in management accounting—A nursing perspective. *Advances in Management Accounting*, 29: 127–181.

Wankhade, P. (2021). A 'journey of personal and professional emotions': Emergency ambulance professionals during COVID-19. *Public Money & Management*. https://doi.org/10.1080/09540962.2021.2003101.

Wankhade, P., Heath, G., and Radcliffe, J. (2018). Cultural change and perpetuation in organisations: Evidence from an English emergency ambulance service. *Public Management Review*, 20(6): 923–948.

Wankhade, P., and Mackway-Jones, K. (eds.). (2015). *Ambulance Services: Leadership and Management Perspectives*. New York: Springer.

Wankhade, P., McCann, L., and Murphy, P. (eds.). (2019). *Critical Perspectives on the Management and Organization of Emergency Services*. Abingdon: Routledge.

Wankhade, P., and Murphy, P. (2012). Bridging the theory and practice gap in emergency services research: Case for a new journal. *International Journal of Emergency Services*, 1(1): 4–9.

Wankhade, P., Stokes, P., Tarba, S., and Rodgers, P. (2020). Work intensification and ambidexterity—the notions of extreme and 'everyday' experiences in emergency contexts: Surfacing dynamics in the ambulance service. *Public Management Review*, 22(1): 48–74.

Weber, M. (1904). *The Protestant Ethic and the Spirit of Capitalism*. New York: Charles Schribner's Sons.

Wylie, R. (ed.). (2020). *Public Value Management: Institutional Design and Decision for the Common Good*. Lanham, MD: Rowman & Littlefield.

2 Working towards attaining professional status

Introduction and background

Professional forms of relationships and organisations are interwoven into the social fabric of all advanced societies, with the capacity to advance, develop, and change character (Ackroyd, 1996; Abbott, 1988; Larson, 1977). While their origin dates back to the late 17th century (Burrage et al., 1990), the formation of modern professional associations including that of doctors, lawyers, accountants, engineers, etc., did not occur until the middle or end of the 19th century, for example, the British Medical Association was formed only in 1854 (Ackroyd, 1996; Perkin, 1989). In comparison to modern organisations, these structures were often organised like the medieval guilds, in a cellular fashion with a central council (Ackroyd, 1996). Modern free-standing professions, such as medicine, also have a central organisation, which often has considerable control over education, training and licensing of healthcare professionals and have achieved a degree of 'occupational closure' of the labour market (Ackroyd, 1996: 610).

There has been considerable debate about the sociological meaning of what constitutes a 'profession' (see Fournier, 1999). Parkin (1995)'s contention that professions hold a 'privileged' position in society including a measure of occupational success is generally accepted by social scientists and scholars (Yam, 2004; Muzio et al., 2013). Broad sociological issues such as social stratification and exclusion, poverty and inequality and occupational closure, associated with neoliberal capitalism have been embraced by the debate on professions (Muzio and Kirkpatrick, 2011; Granter et al., 2015) and this growing interest is further enriched by the discourse on the organisational dimensions of extreme work and its management by academics and scholars which has been accompanied by developments in practitioner-based literature (Empson, 2007; Maister, 1997; Ackroyd, 1996).

Professional work is changing because of technology, innovation, greater inter-professional collaboration, and new professional standards. Modern

DOI: 10.4324/9781003198017-2

organisations are more connected and less isolated and recent debates have discussed the emergence of new forms of professionalism within the changing organisational and societal contexts, a kind of 'hybridisation' in professional work as against the traditional dualistic and oppositional understanding of professionalism set against managerialism in work and organisational settings (McCann and Granter, 2019; Noordegraaf, 2015; Besharov and Smith, 2012; Blomgren and Waks, 2015; Loewenstein, 2014). Such a view focuses on three principles or questions—how work is *coordinated*; how *authority* is established, and what *values* are at stake (see Noordegraaf, 2015: 189).

It has been argued that for an occupation to be recognised as profession, it should possess certain traits which are applied along a continuum of professionalism for each occupation (Goode, 1960; Yam, 2004). These include (i) an extensive theoretical knowledge base; (ii) a legitimate expertise in a specialised field; (iii) an altruistic commitment to service; (iv) an unusual degree of autonomy in work; (v) a code of ethics and conduct overseen by a body of representatives from within the field itself; and (vi) a personal identity that stems from the professional's occupation (Yam, 2004: 979). Although it is necessary to note that a trait-based approach to measuring professionalisation is not immune from criticism within the sociological literature (see Forsyth, 1994) and such attributes are seen as serving self-interest, representing professional ideology without a supporting theoretical framework (Saks, 1983). This is particularly pertinent in case of nursing and its claim to be a true profession (see Yam, 2004). Wilensky's (1964) influential paper, titled '*The Professionalisation of Everyone*' captured this criticism. Nevertheless, formal knowledge is considered as a cornerstone of professionalisation in the sociology of professions literature (Freidson, 1986). We will 'test' some of these attributes in the case of the three emergency services later in this chapter.

There is a growing academic interest, among business and management scholars, in a systematic and critical understanding of 'work' and 'professionalism' within the context of specific organisational settings, both within private firms and within publicly funded services and organisations; Muzio et al., 2013; Lounsbury and Ventresca, 2003; Brint, 1994; McCann and Granter, 2019). This focus on the organisational context of professional development is well developed in academic literature, including various attempts to colonise and harness organisational spaces, processes and policies (Muzio and Kirkpatrick, 2011; Muzio et al., 2011; Muzio et al., 2007; Ackroyd, 1996). An institutional perspective to understanding the development of professions and the process of professional change is also prevalent (see Muzio et al., 2013).

The next section will therefore describe and critically analyse the growing research interest in the sociobiological understanding of the origins and development of these 'professional' activities within the context of the emergency services.

The state of 'blue-collar' professionalism

In our previous work, we have argued that notwithstanding the global provision of emergency services, a systematic and critical understanding of its working, organisations and workforce is still evolving (Wankhade and Murphy, 2012; Wankhade and Weir, 2015; Wankhade and Mackway-Jones, 2015; Murphy and Greenhalgh, 2018).

In policing, there is a substantial body of criminological work examining issues around culture(s), autonomy, leadership, discretion, and governance (Loftus, 2009; Moskos, 2008; Raine, 2015). More recent work has examined issues around equality, diversity, and changing cultural perspectives, the meaning of professionalism and identity within policing (Flanagan, 2008; Reiner, 1978, 2010; Holdaway, 1983, 2017; Charman, 2017, 2019). Equivalent research on ambulance and paramedics has focused on work intensity, extremes, targets, performance, identity, and culture (Metz, 1981; McCann et al., 2013; Wankhade, 2012, 2011; Tangherlini, 1998; Granter et al., 2019). The sociological research on fire and rescue services is more limited, focusing on leadership and governance, industrial relations, masculinity, emotions, risks, and technology (Murphy et al., 2020; Murphy and Greenhalgh, 2018; Tracy and Scott, 2006). However, organisational research connecting to the broader body of work examining the sociological understanding of professions and professional work is currently limited (Kirkpatrick and Ackroyd, 2003; Joseph and Alex, 1972).

McCann and Granter (2019: 2) suggest that uniformed, mobile, and technical occupations, such as emergency services (even nursing), have not traditionally enjoyed a high status within the 'hierarchy of professions' (Abbot, 1988) and at best, have been seen as 'semi' or 'para' professions, having never acquired the full traits of a profession (Ackroyd, 1996) including an 'exclusionary social closure', a kind of licence to operate to the exclusion of other groups. This includes, amongst other things, control over their knowledge base, self-regulation, autonomy and formal training and educational pathways (Muzio et al., 2013). While this may be true at least to some extent in the past, there are several positive developments around these features offering fresh insights into a more systematic understanding of professional work in these organisations.

Before we examine them in further detail, it is necessary and pertinent to discuss the changing context of the emergency services in order to appreciate the growth of these services as professions.

Changing emergency services context

In our earlier works, we have examined the changing context of the emergency services globally and more specifically in the U.K. We have reported how emergency services globally are dealing with complex societal pressures such as ageing populations, demographic changes, and other sociocultural factors, while coping up with significant cuts in operational budgets and increasing demand for their services (Wankhade et al., 2019). In response to these challenges, some emergency service organisations are adopting new public management (NPM) style reform features. Evermore 'efficiency and 'effectiveness' is pursued through better job designs, contracting out of back room functions, greater inter-agency collaboration, and the use of technology as organisations seek to be more 'resilient' while maintaining their emergency preparedness as first responders in dealing with any emergency (Wankhade and Patnaik, 2019; McCann and Granter, 2019). The growing hybridity of inter-agency work and the interplay between the professional and the managerial aspects of their work have made this analysis more meaningful and timelier (Noordegraaf, 2015; Currie et al., 2016). The COVID-19 pandemic spotlighted the interoperability aspect of their working, something which we will return to in Chapter 3.

However, significant changes in the operational and policy landscapes are resulting in additional questions about the core function and responsibilities of these services. The traditional meaning of a sudden, unexpected, and dangerous situation resulting in an '*emergency*' are also shifting. McCann and Granter (2019) point to a range of issues now being tackled by these services which reflect societal inequalities, drug abuse, the housing and social care crisis, and hospital overcrowding amongst other things. Structural, organisational and cultural issues are influencing both the direction of travel and the pace of change although it would be incorrect to assume that the pace of change or the nature of some of the changes being implemented or proposed are unform or consistent across the three main emergency services (Murphy et al., 2020). It is worth pointing out that the nomenclature of the emergency services is also context specific in different societal settings (e.g., ambulance provision is often provided by fire crews in North America and Continent Europe). However, what is common across these services is the fundamental shift in the nature of demand, the scope of the work, and the nature of service delivery over the last decade, which has influenced the pursuit of reforms, the services response, and the debate over greater professionalisation. A brief review of the 'professionalisation journey' of the three services is provided to illustrate the organisational and professional working of these main emergency services.

The state of professionalisation in the ambulance, police, and fire and rescue services

Having provided some brief introduction to the changing context, this section critically analyses the state of professionalisation in the three main services. We start with the ambulance services, followed by the police and fire and rescue services.

Ambulance services

The relatively recent historical evolution of the ambulance service from a simple patient transport service requiring just a driving licence and a first-aid certificate, delivering sick and injured patients to hospital emergency departments (EDs) as quickly as possible on a 'scoop and run' basis, into a modern, mobile prehospital care provider is nothing short of a transformational process (Pollock, 2015, 2013; Newton and Harris, 2015; Newton and Hodge, 2012; Department of Health, 2005). This transformation has been aided by the enhanced clinical skills of frontline paramedics resulting into more interventions; and more options to treat the patients on the scene including 'see and treat' and 'hear and treat' options resulting into fewer journeys to the overcrowded hospital emergency departments (Wankhade et al., 2020; National Audit Office NAO, 2017, 2011). Significant policy and professional changes have facilitated this process in the U.K. For instance, the Health and Care Professionals Council (HCPC), which sets standards for Allied Health Professions in the U.K., has required a 'Bachelor's degree with Honours' for new paramedic registration from September 2021 (See Givati et al., 2018). The College of Paramedics, which is the recognised professional body for paramedics, is now seeking a *Royal College* status for the recognition of the professional expertise of paramedics, while witnessing a steady rise in its membership. The central role played by the ambulance service in the Urgent and Emergency Care strategy is now acknowledged in policy reports (Association of Ambulance Chief Executives, 2020; Carter, 2018; NAO, 2017, 2011; House of Commons, 2017).

Similar initiatives to enhance the status of the profession are also happening elsewhere. In Australia, paramedic registration became mandatory in December 2018 while in neighbouring New Zealand, paramedics are now formally recognised, and all practising paramedics must be registered as of 1 August 2021. In the U.S., the American Paramedic Association launched a *Paramedic Manifesto* in April 2019 setting a new agenda for the future of the discipline of paramedicine driven by its professional paramedic members. The National Registry (established in 1970) maintains the accreditation for paramedics and other grades and over 400,000 individuals are currently nationally certified at the Emergency Medical Responder (EMR), Emergency Medical Technician (EMT), advanced-EMT (AEMT), or Paramedic level. Similarly in Canada and Ireland, paramedicine is now a regulated profession. The position in Europe is also changing with new national regulations and laws, and in most countries, pre-hospital care is partly funded by the government (Bos et al., 2015). Not surprisingly, there are growing calls for harmonisation of the paramedic education on an European level and the need for at least a bachelor's degree university education (Duason et al., 2021).

Ten years ago, in their study of U.K. paramedics, McCann et al. (2013) presented a rather 'bleak' account of the state of affairs. Adopting Metz (1981)'s description of ambulance paramedics and technicians as 'blue-collar professionals', they highlighted a series of challenges facing the professionalisation agenda. These included the organisational and performance pressures faced by frontline crews, their remarkable persistence in the quest for greater autonomy and greater scope of practise, and the limited success of the institutional entrepreneurship of the College of Paramedics. There is some resonance in the issues raised by McCann et al. (2013) and other studies have focused on the single-minded focus on response time-based performance targets; the work intensity of frontline ambulance crews and the dysfunctional effect on staff health and wellbeing and organisational delivery (see Snooks et al., 2009; Siriwardena et al., 2010; Wankhade, 2011, 2016; Wankhade et al., 2018; Granter et al., 2019; Wankhade, 2021). The arguments for the ever-rising ambulance 999 demand and funding gap are also well rehearsed (NAO, 2017; Wankhade et al., 2020, 2016). It is worth pointing out that in their subsequent analysis, McCann and Granter (2019) acknowledged that their previous characterisation of the ambulance professionalisation project was rather 'downbeat' and presented a more positive account of the professionalisation of ambulance paramedics, but they did not anticipate the speed of more recent changes, or the impact of the pandemic.

Policing

Globally, the police services are also confronted with a range of challenges not traditionally within their remit. These include dealing with espionage, cyber-crime, child and sexual exploitation, gun and drug-related cases in addition to dealing with local crimes such as robbery, burglary, and assault (Wankhade and Patnaik, 2019; Wankhade and Weir, 2015). The COVID-19 pandemic further resulted in additional powers (and responsibility) being given to police to restrict and/or prohibit events, detain people and enforce government announced lockdowns and quarantine restrictions across the world. The widespread use of surveillance technology and the use of drones for enforcing social distancing and quarantine raise serious concerns around individual liberty and human rights. Policing has always enjoyed an ambiguous some would say 'love/hate' relationship with citizens in contrast to the other two services due to the nature of their job and their power to arrest people.

In England, there are 43 territorial police forces that operate and are funded locally with policy and oversight from the Home Office at the national government level. Although policing collectively employs one of the largest publicly funded workforces, its professionalisation journey has been influenced by a series of factors. The changing social landscapes of policing has also contributed to the pace of reforms (Charman, 2019) and non-crime-related incidences account for almost 82% of 'command and control' calls (College of Policing, 2015). Police forces are now called to deal with 'new and novel' forms of crime relating to child sexual exploitation, domestic slavery, human trafficking, and cybercrime (Wankhade and Patnaik, 2019), with the emphasis of police activities on managing risk, harm, vulnerability and safeguarding and less on 'fraud and fighting crime' (Charman, 2019).

As mentioned earlier in this chapter the vast majority of criminology literature has not engaged with the sociological literature of professions (Fleming, 2014; Sklansky, 2014) and even less with the contemporary context of claims of a profession (Holdaway, 1983; Holdaway, 2019). Descriptions of the police as a profession have differed over time but were first raised in late 1960s when the History of the Police in England and Wales (Critchley, 1967) was published and again in 1970s when the issue of integrity and accountability was highlighted as a hallmark of professionalism (Mark, 1977). Further claims to professional status, focusing on educational qualifications, managerial competence of senior managers and direct entry to officer rank were then added (Holdaway, 2017). More recently Neyroud (2011) argued for establishing a professional body, a more evidence-based approach to practice and continuous professional development in the claim for being a profession. The College of Policing was set up in 2013, as professional body across policing but as an operationally independent arm's-length body of the Home Office. Police Reform and Social Responsibility Act, 2011 led to the introduction of directly elected Police and Crime Commissioners (PCCs) to replace Police Authorities, representing a significant change in the governance of policing. The PCCs became responsible for setting local priorities, budgets, and scrutinising service delivery although considerable debate remains exists about the real value or added value of their role and contribution (Lister and Rowe, 2014; Lister, 2014; Raine, 2015).

Key issues around authority and power are also considered central to claims of professionalism (Johnson, 1972) though the notion that police identity is uniform across ranks has been challenged and attracts considerable criticism (Cordner, 2017; Waddington, 1999; Loftus, 2009, 2010; see Evetts, 2011, for distinction between professionalism from above and below). Nevertheless, a strong sense of 'identity' still prevails within lower ranked officers, characterised by a 'common sense' approach and 'speed' against a more considered, evidence-based approach of executive ranks (Constable, 2017; see Westmarland and Rowe, 2018 on the difference in attitudes to ethics by senior and junior ranks).

Claims for 're-professionalisation' of the police services have also been met with some scepticism not least in its opposition from the lower ranks (Lumsden, 2017; Holdaway, 2019). Some of the confusion centres around the extent and limits of the policing role and Millie (2013) draws the distinction between 'wide and narrow' policing at the frontline. In her study of new police recruits Charman (2017) found growing 'cynicism' to be a result of the increasing gap between expectations and the reality of a job that is mediated in a climate of changing police priorities, workload/resource pressures, and budgetary cuts (NAO, 2015a).

Some success has, however, been achieved in developing new educational programmes for police forces through the introduction of Policing Education Qualifications Framework (PEQF) in 2016. Focusing on new recruits, it requires them to complete a police constable degree apprenticeship and a degree programme in policing in conjunction with Higher Education Institutions but concerns persist about attracting recruits from the Black, Asian and Minority Ethnic (BAME) and other socially challenged communities (Tong and Halenberg, 2017). The key question which clouds the question of police professionalisation in the U.K. still centres around the unresolved debate about what the role of policing in modern society is and what is the appropriate balance between police legitimacy, crime reduction, and public expectations.

Fire and rescue services

The fire and rescue services (FRS) present a unique challenge in terms of the multiplicity of their organisational models and service delivery. In North America, the FRS are often the first responders to the emergency 911 calls, with the paramedic crews (and sometimes police) accompanying the firefighters. In many European countries, they are delivered as part of public-private initiatives. Even in the U.K., where they are publicly funded, there are different governance models for the 44 FRS operating in England, the 3 in Wales and 1 each in Scotland and Northern Ireland (Murphy and Greenhalgh, 2018) all operating under a climate of fiscal austerity (NAO, 2015b).

Globally, FRS are witnessing significant changes in the rate of fire incidences and deaths, notwithstanding the increasing complexity of major incidents such as the Grenfell Tower Fire (2017) in London and wildfires in Australia, Europe, the U.S. and more recently the U.K. In the U.K., the number of fire-related call-outs is down by almost 40% in the last 10 years (NAO, 2015b), in contrast to the number of call-outs to traffic accidents which are increasing and the increasing demand on their protective and prevention services. Significant issues such as variability of service provision, the lack of diversity in the workforce, and the lack of operational freedom for fire leaders remain unresolved and have been highlighted as national areas of key concerns in successive 'State of the Fire and Rescue Services' reports from Her Majesty's Chief Inspector of Fire and Rescue Services (HMICFRS, 2020, 2021). The introduction of Police and Fire and

Crime Commissioners in England has encouraged greater collaboration and interoperability with the police in England whereas the pandemic and the devolved administrations in Scotland and Wales have encouraged greater collaboration and interoperability with the NHS. Mansfield (2015) suggests this may require them to make a strategic choice to either confine itself to putting out fires and 'lose its brand' or expand on its growing preventive role in collaboration with other emergency and public services.

Compared to the ambulance and police services, attempts at professionalisation in the U.K. FRS have been relatively perfunctory, missing at least two key elements for being called a 'profession'. First, unlike the ambulance and police services, it lacks an autonomous, arm's length professional body, akin to the College of Police or the College of Paramedics to regulate professional training and education. Second and crucially, there are no nationally agreed entry requirements for fire fighters or a requirement for a university-level degree or equivalent qualification. A similar situation prevails in other countries such as the U.S., Australia, Canada and Europe, where applicants require only a high school diploma and demonstrate high levels of physical fitness to work as a firefighter, although an increasing number of firefighters do undertake undergraduate and postgraduate degrees to advance their careers.

A firefighter job has traditionally been characterised as being physical, the role is dominated by men and places a huge regard on team or group membership (Yarnal et al., 2004; Andrews and Ashworth, 2018). Some accounts portray firefighting (and firefighters) as a 'masculine form of heroism' (Yarnal et al., 2004: 686), or describe how firefighters develop a disposition to risk taking in their careers (see Desmond, 2011) although this characterisation is increasingly outdated (Eyre, 2018). Similarly in their study of the U.S. firefighters, O'Neill et al. (2017) present the notion of 'masculine emotional culture' highlighting the twin emotions of joviality and companionate love. In another American study, Tracy and Scott (2006: 6) demonstrate 'how discourses of occupational prestige and masculine heterosexuality allow firefighters to frame their work in preferred, privileged terms'. More recently Wankhade and Patnaik (2019) find a few similarities with the U.K. context with its lack of gender and racial diversity in the workforce and the group camaraderie, reflected in the *Watch* culture (See also Chetkovich, 1997).

Having highlighted the contemporary issues in the professionalisation in each of the emergency services work, the final part of the chapter critically analyses respectively their claim to be deemed as 'professionals'.

How professional are the emergency services?

The previous section has looked at the journey of the three emergency services in their quest to be deemed as professional occupations in the context of the definitions and debates in the sociological literature on professions.

However, as our analysis suggests, an inconsistent picture emerges around the nature and scope of such reforms in a highly complex and dynamic environment.

Emergency services are closely connected with some of the key attributes which are traditionally associated with the 'traits' of a profession. These include a sense of occupational closure (in the form of a licence to practice their occupation); a high degree of autonomy in their work and an altruistic commitment to public service (Muzio et al., 2013). However, as we have argued in the preceding sections, there are serious and new pressures affecting these attributes. The notion of 'occupational closure' is increasingly being challenged by market forces and competitive pressures to bring people from external jurisdictions. While FRS have few recruitment issues as the workforce contracts, the U.K. NHS ambulance services are facing a national shortage of paramedics as they compete with private providers (offering better pay and working conditions) and alternative recruitment options for NHS paramedics to work in the primary and social care settings (NAO, 2017; Wankhade et al., 2020; McCann and Granter, 2019). The police and FRS are also facing growing calls to open their recruitment of senior ranks to outside candidates to bring greater balance and diversity in leadership roles. The notion of professional autonomy is being seriously challenged by operational pressures in a climate of fiscal austerity and the primacy of performance metrics (Wankhade et al., 2020). Attempts at organisational cultural change in these heavily operationally focused services have produced mixed results (Wankhade et al., 2018; Charman, 2017; Murphy and Greenhalgh, 2018; HMICFRS, 2020, 2021).

Recent evidence on the contested notion of professional 'identities' especially by junior and frontline staff highlights conflict with the attempts to 'impose' professionalism by senior leadership and professional institutions and are sometimes regarded with 'suspicion' by junior staff (Holdaway, 2019; Charman, 2019; McCann and Granter, 2019; Wankhade et al., 2015). Failure to recruit from BAME groups and being unrepresentative of the communities they serve has been criticised in official reports (House of Commons, 2016; HMICFRS, 2020, 2021). Traditional command and control structures and a hierarchical style of leadership and decision-making, which serve some useful purposes in crisis situations, are increasingly seen (by frontline staff) to be unfit for leading and managing a very diverse work force, particularly if lacking empathy and compassion (Greenberg et al., 2020; Learmonth, 2019), which is something brought to the fore during COVID-19 pandemic. Similarly, demand for greater inter-agency work and blurring professional borders of the first responders (Tehrani and Hesketh, 2019) has questioned, traditional organisational boundaries, calling for more in-depth understanding of the occupational and organisational terrain of these services. Emergency service workers are dealing with host of new issues and challenges which have not been traditionally considered to be in their domain, resulting in some confusion about their core function and duties. McCann and Granter (2019: 222) have argued that the changing nature of the 'core mission' of emergency services and how the 'boundaries between such categories of work as emergency care, primary care, vulnerability, mental health, preparedness, resilience and order-maintenance are in flux'.

The three emergency services still have some way to go in terms of possessing an extensive theoretical knowledge base, given their very different trajectories. For instance, paramedics education in the U.K. has quickly moved to the university graduate degree, which has been greatly assisted by a pro-active stand by the College of Paramedics. The police education programme (PEQF) is merging but is and facing concerns and even cynicism from junior ranks and their associations (Holdaway, 2019; Charman, 2019). The FRS education and training, globally, is still strongly focused on operational requirements and fitness regimes and requires an independent professional body to actively pursue uniform education standards for firefighters to find some balance between classroom and practical learning. Consequently, these organisations are subjected to differing levels of professional standards, codes and oversight, although a Fire Standards Board has recently been set up by the National Fire Chiefs council and the government to 'oversee the identification, organisation, development and maintenance of professional Standards for fire and rescue services in England'. The development of 'institutional entrepreneurship' through professional institutions (McCann et al., 2013) to build on the professionalisation gains in the police and FRS still remains an ambitious and elusive goal.

Conclusion

The above analysis suggests that while emergency services have made great strides in expanding their skills and expertise, their quest to be considered as fully developed professions are still not without challenges. McCann and Granter (2019) have recently pointed to the dangers to professional discretion and autonomy of operating under the current conditions of managerialism, metrics, and marketisation. This is intensifying the risk of 'de-professionalisation' as a climate of fiscal austerity is more likely to generate a demand for 'compliance' that will restrict discretion. We have also argued elsewhere how a growing funding-gap is resulting into additional pressure on staff recruitment, training, and education opportunities amidst increasing attempts of out-sourcing and competitive pressures (Wankhade et al., 2020; McCann and Granter, 2019; Murphy et al., 2019). Our analysis has highlighted how new or additional pressures on autonomy, representative membership, and oversight of these institutions are precluding or hampering the development and imposition of new professional standards.

This calls for an ambitious research agenda, encouraging scholars, and practitioners working in the field of emergency management and those interested in the sociology of professions, to actively collaborate to research these organisations and explore and make sense of the meaning of 'professionalisation' within the context of the changing socio-economic realities and the emergence of new, novel, and hybrid organisational forms.

References

Abbott, A. (1988). *The System of Professions: An Essay on the Division of Expert Labor.* Chicago: University of Chicago Press.

Ackroyd, S. (1996). Organisation contra organisation: Professions and organisational change in the United Kingdom. *Organization Studies,* 17(4): 599–621.

Andrews, R., and Ashworth, R. (2018). Feeling the heat? Management reform and workforce diversity in the English fire service. In P. Murphy and G. Greenhalgh (eds.), *Fire and Rescue Services: Leadership and Management Perspectives,* 145–158. Geneva: Springer.

Association of Ambulance Chief Executives (AACE). (2020). *Annual Report-2020–21.* London: AACE.

Besharov, M.L., and Smith, W.K. (2012). *Multiple Logics Within Organizations: An Integrative Framework and Model of Organizational Hybridity.* Ithaca, NY: Cornell University Working Blomgren, M., and Waks, C. (2015). Coping with contradictions: Hybrid professionals managing institutional complexity. *Journal of Professions and Organization,* 2(1): 78–102 .

Bos, N., Krol, M., Veenvliet, C. and Plass, A.M. (2015). *Ambulance care in Europe: Organization and practices of ambulance services in 14 European countries.* Nivel: Netherlands. ISBN 978-94-6122-368-5.

Brint, S.G. (1994). *In an Age of Experts: The Changing Role of Professionals in Politics and Public Life.* Princeton, NJ: Princeton University Press.

Burrage, M., Jaraush, K., and Siegrist, H. (1990). An actor based framework for the study of professionalism. In M. Burrage and R. Torstendahl (eds.), *The Professions in Theory and History.* London: Routledge.

Carter, L. (2018). *Operational Productivity and Performance in English NHS Ambulance Trusts: Unwarranted Variations.* London: Stationery Office.

Charman, S. (2017). *Police Socialisation, Identity and Culture: Becoming Blue.* Basingstoke: Palgrave.

Charman, S. (2019). Changing landscapes, changing identities—Policing in England and Wales. In P. Wankhade, L. McCann, and P. Murphy (eds.), *Critical Perspectives on the Management and Organization of Emergency Services.* Abingdon: Routledge.

Chetkovich, C. (1997). *Real Heat: Gender and Race in the Urban Fire Service.* New Brunswick, NJ: Rutgers University Press.

College of Policing. (2015). *Estimating Demand on the Police Service. Coventry: College of Policing.* Available at: www.college.police.uk/News/Collegenews/Documents/Demand%20Report%2023_1_15_noBleed.pdf

Constable, N. (2017). *Canary in the Mine.* Available at: https://nathanconstable.wordpress.com/2017/11/03/canary-in-the-mine/

Cordner, G. (2017). Police culture: Individual and organizational differences in police officer Perspectives. *Policing: An International Journal of Police Strategies & Management*, 40(1): 11–25.

Critchley, T. (1967). *A History of the Police in England and Wales.* London: Constable.

Currie, G., Burgess, N., and Tuck, P. (2016). The (un)desirability of hybrid managers as 'controlled' professionals: Comparative cases of tax and healthcare professionals. *Journal of Professions and Organization*, 3(2): 142–153.

Department of Health DH. (2005). *Taking Healthcare to the Patients: Transforming NHS Ambulance Services.* London: Department of Health.

Desmond, M. (2011). Making firefighters deployable. *Qualitative Sociology*, 34(1): 59–77.

Dúason, S., Ericsson, C., Jónsdóttir, H.L., Andersen, J.V. and Andersen, T.L. (2021). European paramedic curriculum—a call for unity in paramedic education on a European level. *Scandinavian Journal of Trauma, Resuscitation and Emergency Medicine*, 29, 72.

Empson, L. (2007). *Managing the Modern Law Firm.* Oxford: Oxford University Press.

Evetts, J. (2011). A new professionalism? Challenges and opportunities. *Current Sociology*, 59: 406–422.

Eyre, A. (2018). The Making of a Hero: An Exploration of Heroism in Disasters and Implications for the Emergency Services. In Murphy, P. and Greenhalgh, K. (eds). *Fire and Rescue Services: Leadership and Management Perspectives.* pp. 113–130. New York: Springer.

Flanagan, R. (2008). *Review of Policing: Final Report.* London: HMSO.

Fleming, J. (2014). The pursuit of professionalism: Lessons from Australia. In J.M. Brown (eds.), *The Future of Policing*, 355–368. London: Routledge.

Forsyth, S. (1994). Theorizing in the sociology of the professions: relevance for nursing. In J. Germov (eds.), *Health Papers: Presented at the 'Social Theory in Practice' TASA Conference.* Department of Sociology and Anthropology, 124–133. Newcastle: University of Newcastle.

Fournier, V. (1999). The appeal to 'professionalism' as a disciplinary mechanism. *The Sociological Review*, 47(2): 280–307.

Freidson, E. (1986). *Professional Powers: A Study of the Institutionalization of Formal Knowledge.* Chicago: University of Chicago Press.

Givati, A., Markham, C., and Street, K. (2018). The bargaining of professionalism in emergency care practice: NHS paramedics and higher education. *Advances in Health Sciences Education*, 23: 353–369.

Goode, W. (1960). Encroachment, charlatanism, and the emerging profession: Psychology, sociology and medicine. *American Sociological Review*, 25(6): 902–914.

Granter, E., McCann, L., and Boyle, M. (2015). Extreme work/normal work: Intensification, storytelling, and hypermediation in the (re)construction of 'the new normal'. *Organization*, 22: 443–456.

Granter, E., Wankhade, P., McCann, L., Hassard, J., and Hyde, P. (2019). Multiple dimensions of work intensity: Ambulance work as edgework. *Work Employment and Society*, 33(2): 280–297.

Greenberg, N., Docherty, M., Gnanapragasam, S., and Wessely, S. (2020). Managing mental health challenges faced by healthcare workers during COVID-19 pandemic. *British Medical Journal*. 368. http://doi.org/10.1136/bmj.m1211

Heath, G., Wankhade, P., and Murphy, P. (2021). Exploring the wellbeing of ambulance staff using the 'public value' perspective: Opportunities and challenges for research. *Public Money & Management* (early cite). http://doi.org/10.1080/0954 0962.2021.1899613

Her Majesty's Inspectorate of Constabulary and Fire and Rescue Services, HMIC-FRS. (2020). *State of Fire and Rescue—The Annual Assessment of Fire and Rescue Services in England 2020*. London: Stationery Office.

Her Majesty's Inspectorate of Constabulary and Fire and Rescue Services, HMIC-FRS. (2021). *State of Fire and Rescue—The Annual Assessment of Fire and Rescue Services in England 2021*. London: Stationery Office.

Holdaway, S. (1983). *Inside the British Police: A Force at Work*. Oxford: Blackwell.

Holdaway, S. (2017). The re-professionalization of the police in England and Wales. *Criminology & Criminal Justice*, 17(5): 588–604.

Holdaway, S. (2019). The professionalisation of the police in England and Wales: A critical appraisal. In P. Wankhade, L. McCann, and P. Murphy (eds.), *Critical Perspectives on the Management and Organization of Emergency Services*. Abingdon: Routledge.

House of Commons. (2016). *Police Diversity: First Report of Session 2016–17, HC 27. House of Commons Home Affairs Committee*. London: Stationery Office.

House of Commons Committee of Public Accounts. (2017). *NHS Ambulance Services*. London: House of Commons. Available at: www.parliament.uk/business/committees/committees-az/commons-select/public-accounts-committee/inquiries/parliament-2015/ambulance-servicesstudy-16-17/

Johnson, T.J. (1972). *Professions and Power*. London: Macmillan.

Joseph, N., and Alex, N. (1972). The uniform: A sociological perspective. *American Journal of Sociology*, 77(4): 719–730.

Kirkpatrick, I., and Ackroyd, S. (2003). Archetype theory and the changing professional organisation: A critique and alternative. *Organization*, 10(4): 731–750.

Larson, M.S. (1977). *The Rise of Professionalism: A Sociological Analysis*. Berkeley, CA: University of California Press.

Learmonth, M. (2019). Rethinking the new 'leadership' mainstream: An historical perspective from the National health service. In P. Wankhade, L. McCann, and P. Murphy (eds.), *Critical Perspectives on the Management and Organization of Emergency Services*. Abingdon: Routledge.

Lister, S. (2014). Scrutinising the role of the police and crime panel in the new era of police governance in England and Wales. *Safer Communities*, 13(1): 22–31.

Lister, S., and Rowe, M. (2014). Electing police and crime commissioners in England and Wales: Prospecting for the democratisation of policing. *Policing and Society*, 25(4): 358–377.

Loewenstein, J. (2014). Take my word for it: How professional vocabularies foster organizing. *Journal of Professions and Organization*, 1(1): 65–83.

Loftus, B. (2009). *Police Culture in a Changing World*. Oxford: Oxford University Press.

Loftus, B. (2010). Police occupational culture: Classic themes, altered times. *Policing and Society*, 20(1): 1–20.

Lounsbury, M., and Ventresca, M. (2003). The new structuralism in organization theory. *Organization*, 10(3): 457–480.

Lumsden, K. (2017). It's a profession, it isn't a job': Police officers' views on the professionalisation of policing in England. *Sociological Research Online*, 22(3): 4–20.

Maister, D.H. (1997). *Managing the Professional Service Firm*. New York: Free Press.

Mansfield, C. (2015). *Fire Works: A Collaborative Way Forward for the Fire and Rescue Service*. London: New Local Government Network (NLGN).

Mark, R. (1977). *Policing a Perplexed Society*. London: George, Allen and Unwin.

McCann, L., and Granter, E. (2019). Beyond 'blue-collar professionalism': Continuity and change in the professionalization of uniformed emergency services work. *Journal of Professions and Organizations*, 6(3): 213–232.

McCann, L., Granter, E., Hyde, P., and Hassard, J. (2013). Still blue-collar after all these years? An ethnography of the professionalization of emergency ambulance work. *Journal of Management Studies*, 50: 750–776.

Metz, D.L. (1981). *Running Hot: Structure and Stress in Ambulance Work*. Cambridge, MA: ABT Books.

Millie, A. (2013). The policing task and the expansion (and contraction) of British policing. *Criminology and Criminal Justice*, 13(2): 143–160.

Moskos, P. (2008). *Cop in the Hood: My Year Policing Baltimore's Eastern District*. Princeton: Princeton University Press.

Murphy, P., and Greenhalgh, K. (eds.). (2018). *Fire and Rescue Services: Leadership and Management Perspectives*. New York: Springer.

Murphy, P., Wankhade, P., and Lakoma, K. (2020). The strategic and operational landscape of emergency services in the UK. *International Journal of Emergency Services*, 9(1): 69–88.

Muzio, D., Ackroyd, S., and Chanlat, J.F. (eds.). (2007). *Redirections in the Study of Expert Labour: Established Professions and New Expert Occupations*. Basingstoke: Palgrave.

Muzio, D., Brock, D.M., and Suddaby, R. (2013). Professions and institutional change: Towards an institutional sociology of the professions. *Journal of Management Studies*, 50: 699–721.

Muzio, D., and Kirkpatrick, I. (2011). Professions and organizations—a conceptual framework. *Current Sociology*, 59(4): 389–405.

Muzio, D., Kirkpatrick, I., and Kipping, M. (2011). Professions, organizations and the state: Applying the sociology of the professions to the case of management consultancy. *Current Sociology*, 59(4): 389–405.

National Audit Office (NAO). (2011). *Transforming NHS Ambulance Services*. London: Stationery Office.

National Audit Office. (2015a). *Financial Sustainability of Police Forces in England and Wales*. Available at: www.nao.org.uk/wp-content/uploads/2015/06/Financial-sustainability-of-policeforces.pdf

National Audit Office. (2015b). *Impact of Funding Reductions on Fire and Rescue Services*. Available at: www.nao.org.uk/report/impact-of-funding-reductions-on-fire-and-rescue-services/

National Audit Office. (2017). *NHS Ambulance Services*. London: National Audit Office.

Newton, A., and Harris, G. (2015). Leadership and system thinking in the modern ambulance service. In P. Wankhade and K. Mackway-Jones (eds.), *Ambulance Services: Leadership and Management Perspectives*, 81–94. New York: Springer.

Newton, A., and Hodge, D. (2012). The ambulance service: The past, present and future. *Journal of Paramedic Practice*, 4(5): 303–305.

Neyroud, P. (2011). *Review of Police Leadership and Training*. London: Home Office. Available at: www.gov.uk/government/publications/police-leadership-and-training-report-review

Noordegraaf, M. (2015). Hybrid professionalism and beyond. (New) forms of public professionalism in changing organizational and societal contexts. *Journal of Professions and Organizations*, 2(2): 187–206

O'Neill, O.A., and Rothbard, N.P. (2017). Is love all you need? The effects of emotional culture, suppression, and work-family conflict on firefighter risk-taking and health. *Academy of Management Journal*, 60(1): 78–108.

Parkin, P.A.C. (1995). Nursing the future: A re-examination of the professionalization thesis in the light of some recent developments. *Journal of Advance Nursing*, 21(3): 561–567.

Perkin, H. (1989). *The Professionalisation or English Society 1880–1980*. London: Routledge.

Pollock, A.C. (2013). Ambulance services in London and Great Britain from 1860 until today: A glimpse of history gleaned mainly from the pages of contemporary journals. *Emergency Medicine Journal*, 30(2): 218–222.

Pollock, A.C. (2015). Historical perspectives in the ambulance service. In P. Wankhade and K. Mackway-Jones (eds.), *Ambulance Services: Leadership and Management Perspectives*, 17–28. New York: Springer.

Raine, J. (2015). Enhancing police accountability in England and Wales: What differences are police and crime commissioners making? In P. Wankhade and D. Weir (eds.), *Police Services: Leadership and Management Perspectives*, 97–114. New York: Springer.

Reiner, R. (1978). *The Blue-Coated Worker*. Cambridge: Cambridge University Press.

Reiner, R. (2010). *The Politics of the Police*, 4th ed. Oxford: Oxford University Press.

Saks, M. (1983). Removing the blinker? A critique of recent contributions to the sociology of professions. *Sociological Review*, 31(1): 1–21.

Siriwardena, A.N., Donohoe, R., and Stephenson, J. (2010). Supporting research and development in ambulance services: Research for better health care in prehospital settings. *Emergency Medicine Journal*, 27(4): 324–326.

Sklansky, D.A. (2014). The promise and perils of police professionalism. In J. Brown (eds.), *The Future of Policing*. London: Routledge.

Snooks, H., Evans, A., Wells, B., Peconi, J., Thomas, M., Woollard, M., Guly, H., Jenkinson, E., Turner, J., and Hartley-Sharpe, C. (2009). What are the highest priorities for research in emergency prehospital care? *Emergency Medicine Journal*, 26(2): 549–550.

Tangherlini, T. (1998). *Talking Trauma: A Candid Look at Paramedics Through Their Tradition of Storytelling*. Jackson: University of Mississippi Press.

Tehrani, N., and Hesketh, I. (2019). The role of psychological screening for emergency service responders. *International Journal of Emergency Services*, 8(1): 4–19.

Tong, S., and Halenberg, K. (2017). Education and the police professionalisation agenda: A perspective from England and Wales. In C. Rogers and B. Frevel (eds.), *Higher Police Education: An International Perspective*. London: Springer International.

Tracy, S.J., and Scott, C. (2006). Sexuality, masculinity, and taint management among firefighters and correctional officers: Getting down and dirty with 'America's Heroes' and the 'scum of law enforcement'. *Management Communication Quarterly*, 20(1): 6–38.

Waddington, P.A.J. (1999). Police (canteen) sub-culture. An appreciation. *British Journal of Criminology*, 39(2): 287–309.

Wankhade, P. (2011). Performance measurement and the UK emergency ambulance service: unintended consequences of the ambulance response time targets. *International Journal of Public Sector Management*, 24(5): 382–402.

Wankhade, P. (2012). Different cultures of management and their relationships with organisational performance: evidence from the UK ambulance service. *Public Money & Management*, 32(5): 381–388.

Wankhade, P. (2016). Staff perceptions and changing role of pre-hospital profession in the UK ambulance services: An exploratory study. *International Journal of Emergency Services*, 5(2): 126–144.

Wankhade, P. (2021). A 'journey of personal and professional emotions': Emergency ambulance professionals during COVID-19. *Public Money & Management* (https://doi.org/10.1080/09540962.2021.2003101).

Wankhade, P., Heath, G., and Radcliffe, J. (2018). Cultural change and perpetuation in organisations: Evidence from an English emergency ambulance service. *Public Management Review*, 20(6): 923–948.

Wankhade, P., and Mackway-Jones, K. (eds.). (2015). *Ambulance Services: Leadership and Management Perspectives*. New York: Springer.

Wankhade, P., McCann, L., and Murphy, P. (eds.). (2019). *Critical Perspectives on the Management and Organization of Emergency Services*. New York: Routledge.

Wankhade, P., and Murphy, P. (2012). Bridging the theory and practice gap in emergency services research: Case for a new journal. *International Journal of Emergency Services*, 1(1): 4–9.

Wankhade, P., and Patnaik, S. (2019). *Collaboration and Governance in the Emergency Services: Issues, Opportunities and Challenges*. London: Palgrave Pivot.

Wankhade, P., Stokes, P., Tarba, S., and Rodgers, P. (2020). Work intensification and ambidexterity—the notions of extreme and 'everyday' experiences in emergency contexts: Surfacing dynamics in the ambulance service. *Public Management Review*, 22(1): 48–74

Wankhade, P., and Weir, D. (eds.). (2015). *Police Services: Leadership and Management Perspectives*. New York: Springer.

Westmarland, L., and Rowe, M. (2018). Police ethics and integrity: Can a new code overturn the blue code? *Policing and Society*, 28(7): 854–870.

Wilensky, H.L. (1964). The professionalization of everyone? *American Journal of Sociology*, 70(2): 137–158.

Yam, B. (2004). From vocation to profession: The quest for professionalization of nursing. *British Journal of Nursing*, 13(16): 978–982.

Yarnal, C.M., Dowler, L., and Hutchinson, S. (2004). Don't let the bastards see you sweat: Masculinity, public and private space, and the volunteer firehouse. *Environment and Planning A: Economy and Space*, 36(4): 685–699.

3 Collaboration

Issues, challenges, and opportunities

Introduction

The global pandemic situation, coupled with more recent natural disasters such as forest fires in Australia, Spain, and California and the ongoing security climate and conflicts such as the Ukraine war, have repeatedly shone a spotlight on the contribution of the emergency services within a dynamic and challenging environment. The tight fiscal climate and the continuing demand in the U.K. for maximising efficiencies and reducing cost are generating repeated calls for a more collaborative approach to emergency management beyond major incidents and emergencies. Collaboration is increasingly considered a fundamental aspect of delivering a strong blue-light response (Wankhade and Patnaik, 2019; Murphy et al., 2019). However, recent emergency service response to major incidents such as 9–11 terrorist attacks in New York and Hurricane Katrina in the U.S., the Japanese earthquake and tsunami of 2011, the 2017 Manchester Arena attack and Grenfell Tower fire in London left much to be desired. Various inquiry reports have questioned the level of coordination and cooperation between the emergency services, while highlighting problems around effective joined-up working during these major incidents (see US Government, 2006; Kerslake Report, 2018; Grenfell Inquiry, 2019; Prosser and Taylor, 2020, Zaré and Afrouz, 2012).

In this chapter, we analyse the issues influencing effective collaboration between the emergency services and the current shifts in the interoperability mechanisms and governance architecture, while highlighting some of the challenges. As with previous chapters, we draw upon the available international evidence while focusing on the ambulance, police, and fire and rescue (FRS) services. We contend that successful collaborations between emergency services are contingent upon agile and flexible leadership, institutional conditions under which they are formed, and how such collaborations are managed over time to build, nurture, and support professional and

DOI: 10.4324/9781003198017-3

inter-disciplinary networks. This generates issues around the need for 'quality assurance' which are simultaneously examined.

Understanding the nature of emergency services collaborations

Notwithstanding their stellar role (and sacrifices) in saving lives and property, an objective assessment of the emergency services collaborative efforts and impact is missing in the mainstream management literature (Wankhade and Patnaik, 2019). Several factors contribute to such a research gap.

(i) *Conceptual ambiguity and overlap in the literature* remains one of the key challenges in developing an overarching framework for collaboration. Several scholars of contemporary public management have argued for a collective approach to addressing the so-called persistent 'wicked problems' confronting society since by definition they cannot be addressed by individual actors in isolation (Peters, 1996, 1998; Jones and Thomas, 2007; Crosby and Bryson, 2018; Vangen and Huxham, 2012; Maguire, 2003). However, the use of such wide-ranging terms to refer to the ways to work more collaboratively can make it much more difficult to develop a focused and coherent understanding of collaborations (see Table 3.1). This is particularly true in case of the few specific models developed for emergency services collaborations which tend to use different terminology such as collaboration clusters (Sparf and Petridou, 2018); Public-Private Emergency Collaboration (PPEC) (Diehlmann et al., 2021) or public-safety agency approach (Wilson and Grammich, 2015). Consequently, academics, researchers, and

Table 3.1 Terms of reference for collaboration

Community partnerships	Bolda et al. (2006), El Ansari and Weiss (2006)
Community coalitions	Foster-Fishman et al. (2001)
Collaborative partnerships and networks	Kerka (1997)
Strategic alliances	Langford (2002), Todeva and Knoke (2005), Wankhade and Patnaik (2019)
Stakeholder networks	Szirom et al. (2002)
Collaborative governance	Huxham (2000), Hedlund et al. (2020)
Network governance	Jones et al. (1997)
Advocacy coalition framework (ACF)	Nohrstedt (2013), Weible et al. (2008)

Source: Adapted from Warburton et al. (2008: 471)

practitioners have found it almost impossible to arrive at a shared understanding of the nature of such collaborations or the value they provide. This is a significant problem for the emergency services which routinely deal with disasters, natural hazards, and risks to life and property in a highly unstable and dynamic environment mediated by politics, policy, and budgeting pressures (Wankhade et al., 2019; Wankhade and Patnaik, 2019).

(ii) *Fragmented governance and collaborative frameworks* remain a key stumbling block to a systematic understanding of the functioning of such collaborations (Versrtrepen et al., 2009; Vanneste, 2016; Meyer and Rowan, 1977). Globally, different governance framework between the three main services makes meaningful analysis challenging. For instance, the three main services are largely publicly funded in the U.K. with a few private ambulance providers and they respond to the emergency '999' calls separately once British telecom operator identifies the nature of the emergency and directs the caller to the appropriate respective agency. In North America, the fire services usually are the first responders for emergency '911' calls often having ambulance crews working with them although the practice may differ in different states or municipalities. In Australia, the three services respond separately to the emergency '000' number. Europe has a mixed model of several private-public partnerships across the 27 EU countries for responding to the emergency '112' number using multiple responding scenarios depending upon the nature of the emergency. Structural and cultural barriers including the size and the number of organisations, differences in training regimes and career spines, differences in organisational and professional cultures, resource availability, business models and operating principles, procurement practices among other things are all important influencing factors (Wankhade et al., 2018; Wankhade, 2012; Charman, 2017; Loftus, 2009). Additionally, the lack of robust cost-benefit analysis, hesitance to include private suppliers and multiple institutional arrangements impacting adaptive capacity makes the task more difficult (Weinholt and Andersson, 2015; Diehlmann et al., 2021; Nohrstedt, 2015).

(iii) *Addressing problems of definition, scope and the nature of collaborations* is another challenge. It is neither agreed nor clear as to what such cooperation means or covers nor is there much consistency in defining such multi-agency cooperation. It is commonly addressed as the interoperability between the three mains services, that is, the police, ambulance, and fire services and not some of the more specialised services such as the mountain and cave rescue or coastguards. However, several specialised agencies and organisations such as transport networks, utilities and infrastructure companies, hospitals, local councils, regional bodies, and voluntary organisations are also involved during major incidents (Pitt, 2008). The variability of the emergency/resilience architecture and strategic organisational landscape (Murphy et al., 2020) also impacts on the nature, scale, and scope of a collaborative approach. See Wankhade and Patnaik (2019) for a fuller discussion on the 'top-down' or hard approach such as in the U.S. Federal Emergency Management Agency (FEMA) or the Scottish Resilience model (Scottish Government, 2012) in contrast to the 'bottom-up' models such as the local resilience forums in England (Cabinet Office, 2013) and the paucity of coverage and analysis of such projects in management literature

(iv) *Neo-liberal economic pressures* and market economy-driven factors are forcing emergency services to collaborate while dealing with the roll-out of management-driven standards and partnerships (McCann and Granter, 2019). This has included sharing back-office functions, common use of office and building premises, and resources with little analysis of the intended objectives or cultural change (Wankhade and Patnaik, 2019). The proliferation of NPM-styled reforms in public services including the emergency services is resulting into greater adoption of private sector-styled management practices (Pollitt and Bouckaert, 2017; Brunetto et al., 2022). Reduced public funding and the need to maximise short-term resource efficiency, rather than long-term service effectiveness and outcomes, are currently driving collaborative service delivery. Policy and legislative changes to maximise such gains have also attempted to boost collaborative practices although the evidence for its usefulness is still evolving (Bryson et al., 2015; Vangen et al., 2015. For example, in the U.K., *The Policing and Crime Act 2017* enabled changes to the governance of fire services, allowing the Police and Crime Commissioners (PCCs) to make a business case to run both the police and fire services. This was followed by changes in the police inspection regime to include fire services in their remit and to assess these services on their 'effectiveness, efficiency and how they look after their people' (HMICFRS, 2017).

Scope of emergency interoperability architecture

As argued so far, collaborations are promoted by the policy makers to bring a tangible benefit in terms of policy outcomes. However, such relationships are often ad hoc, short-term and many suffer from high failure rates (see Neisten and Jolink, 2016; Kale and Singh, 2009). Issues adversely impacting effective collaborations include high cost of delivery, limited funding, and lack of strategic planning (Bryson et al., 2006; Grimshaw et al., 2002; Huxham and Vangen, 2005). During large-scale emergency management several other challenges which create problems for multi-agency collaborations have been identified (see Table 3.2).

This analysis suggests that effective emergency collaboration is complex, messy, and contingent on several issues identified earlier. We, however, would like to consider three additional issues which, in our view, are not

Table 3.2 Factors influencing effective collaborations

Eide et al. (2012)	(i) Effective communication within and across emergency agencies; (ii) establishing and maintaining shared situation awareness; and (iii) inter-organisational understanding of structures.
Sparf and Petridou (2018)	(i) Power differentials between agencies and jurisdictions; (ii) mission and cultural conflicts; (ii) role ambiguity; (iv) lack of communications plans; (v) trust between partners; (vi) network density and structure; and (vii) pre-existing relationship
Warburton et al. (2008)	(i) Environment or enabling context; (ii) partner characteristics; (iii) processes, procedures and communication; (iv) structures and relationships; (v) purpose; and (vi) resources
Parry et al. (2015)	(i) Clear and shared vision of collaborative objectives; (ii) trust between collaborating partners; (iii) clear shared resource plan; (iv) robust governance architecture; (v) local cross-party political buy-in and overt support; (vi) organisational differences and legislative barriers; and (vii) realistic timeline and delivery pathway
Wankhade and Patnaik (2019)	(i) Process, structures and governance; (ii) people; and (iii) leadership and culture

entirely appreciated within the collaboration literature and are contingent to the success of any such partnerships. These include (i) role of technology; (ii) emergency logistics; and (iii) challenge of measuring performance

Role of technology in fostering collaboration

As indicated earlier, political and policy attention to emergency preparedness and planning has been rekindled largely by the apparent failure of emergency interoperability during several natural disasters and recent major terrorist responses such as the 9/11 attacks in the U.S. and the London 7/7 bombings (Wankhade and Patnaik, 2019; Lyon, 2003). The National Commission (2004) reported very high casualty rates for first responders at impact zones during the 9/11 attacks and many lives were lost due to lack of use of 'standardised technologies' by participating agencies and services (Bea, 2005; Waugh, 2003; Kapucu, 2005, 2008). In the London bombings, problems with radio communications by the police and other responding agencies in the subway tunnels hampered real-time communication with other agencies (Storm and Eyerman, 2006). Similarly, the decision by the Metropolitan Police Service (MPS) to restrict mobile phone network access to specific users to reduce network traffic and improve first responder access and recovery operations led to the unintended consequence of cutting access to other agencies, including the London Ambulance Service (LAS) thus resulting in considerable worry and distress to families and the general public as they tried to check each other's welfare. This was highlighted in the official reports, prompting the need for developing more resilient telecommunications (Reid and Jowell, 2006; Murphy, 2006). More recently, the Kerslake Inquiry (2018) examined the response of emergency services to the Manchester Arena attack of 2017, and identified a lack of shared communications, coordination and failure of national radio system as areas of major concern and learning.

Literature on the sociology of disasters has highlighted the potential role of technology in responding to such major events but there has not been much research done on the impact of such technology in shaping emergency response (Sanders, 2014; Palen et al., 2009) or how organisational practices shape the use and technology and the ways in which technology alters organisational practices, structures, and response (Manning, 2008; Suchman, 1987). One of the difficulties centres around distinguishing between 'technical' and 'social' issues and treating them as quite separate and distinct identities (Sanders, 2014; Latour, 1991). Sanders (2014: 472) in her ethnographic study of Canadian police, fire, and EMS personnel in rural and urban municipalities, highlighted the differences among the social worlds of the three services and the role and influence of organisational, cultural, and institutional factors, leading to an ideological disconnect between how these technologies were designed for use and their in situ application. Some of the literature on social construction of technology identifies the role and usefulness of stakeholder perception, including job satisfaction of staff, in adopting such technologies by emergency first responders (Agrawal, 2003; Todak et al., 2018). This is particularly relevant to the growing use of technology such as body-worn cameras (BWCs) in policing while conducting raids or dealing with citizens and crowds (Ready and Young, 2015). Adams and Mastracci (2018: 5) found that 'BWCs decrease officers' perceived organizational support, which mediates the relationship between BWCs and burnout' in their study of American police officers. Further empirical research is needed on the role and significance of the social and technological aspects of emergency interoperability (Sanders, 2014).

Sustainable emergency logistics

Effective inter-organisational collaboration in emergency management has been deemed to be the *Holy Grail* for first responders and planners in sharing resources and responding effectively to disasters and emergencies (Verstrepen et al., 2009; Sparf and Petridou, 2018). Despite the lack of consensus in the literature and notwithstanding the theoretical and conceptual ambiguity generated by a multitude of definitions and frameworks, effective collaborations, and a 'networked governance' approach has been considered useful in dealing with contemporary 'wicked 'problems which are multi-causal and without a clear solution but requiring a joint-up effort (Peters, 2015; Sparf and Petridou, 2018). Public management scholars have argued for further empirical research and the need to explore inter-disciplinary links to generate better conceptualisations of collaborative models including the understanding of antecedents, frameworks, variables, and outcomes (Wankhade and Patnaik, 2019; Murphy et al., 2019; Sparf and Petridou, 2018; Blomgren et al., 2008). Bridging the theory-practice gap to encourage co-production of knowledge with practitioners has been a constant refrain of ours in the literature (Wankhade and Murphy, 2012).

The emphasis on effective collaboration is not misplaced. In 2018 alone, natural hazards resulted in more than 10,000 deaths with over 61 million being affected by extreme weather resulting into global annual losses of over $200 billion in the last decade (Diehlmann et al., 2021). It has also been suggested that almost 80% of all relief efforts after disasters are related to logistics (Van Wassenhove, 2006). However, the literature examining the potential of emergency collaboration between government or civil protection agencies is limited (Dienhlmann et al., 2021) although there is a fairly well-developed body of work covering public-private partnership in the public management literature (Barraket et al., 2021; Meurs and Noordegraaf, 2022; Wegner and Verschoore, 2022). Conspicuously, the role and contribution of private firms in disaster coordination including its evaluation is relatively sparse (Balcik et al., 2010; Kapucu et al., 2010; Kapucu et al., 2009; Kapucu and van Wart, 2006). This is a problem if around 75% investment in emergency logistics is expected to come from the private sector (Izumi and Shaw, 2015) and sustainable partnerships have been shown to reduce the burden on the population (Papadopoulos et al., 2017).

Evidence of effective collaboration between the public and private sectors during major incidents is also limited. For instance during Hurricane Katrina, the performance of government agencies including that of FEMA was criticised for a lack of coordinated effort as compared to the quick and professional response of private sector such as Walmart (see Horwitz, 2009; Comfort, 2007; Hicklin et al., 2009). While a fuller discussion on the issues and challenges in effective collaboration between public bodies and private organisations is beyond the scope of this chapter, these include, amongst other things, difference in motivational levels (Gabler et al., 2017); partner selection and reliability (Verdonck, 2017); divergent interests between the partners, varying interest and frequency of such collaborations (Hesselman and Lane, 2017), collaboration resources and performance indicators (Martin et al., 2018) and collaboration stability (Wang and Kopfer, 2011). In their framework, based on logistical and game-theory, Deihlmann et al. (2021) provide further insights into the motivation and incentives of partners including their capacities and resources for successful public-private emergency collaboration (PPEC). Private-public cooperation is thus a great ideal but is hampered by conflicting priorities of the partners.

Measurement challenge in emergency collaborations

The usefulness of collaborations in dealing with crisis and disasters has been discussed extensively in the literature (Bodin, 2017; Lubell, 2013; Newig et al., 2018). However, the literature on empirical evaluation and the variations in performance across such collaborations is more sparse (Nohrstedt, 2015; Wankhade and Patnaik, 2019; Robinson and Gaddis, 2012; Vangen et al., 2015; Bryson et al., 2015; Kelman et al., 2013; Parry et al., 2015). The confusion in the literature around multiple definitions and terminology and the involvement of various private and public configurations of organisations in such collaborations have been already highlighted in section 1 (Mandel and Keast, 2008). Available evidence on the effectiveness of such collaborations is largely confined to the response to major disasters such as Hurricane Katrina, 9/11 or London 7/7 bombings. Further studies to capture different notions of performance to assess collaborative governance, across different phases of the emergency management cycle, have also been called for in the literature (Nohrstedt, 2015; Boin and 'tHart, 2010).

Perspectives on the evaluation of collaborative performance centre around the rationalist modernist and postmodernist perspectives (Nohrstedt, 2015). These two perspectives are distinguished by the aspects of the collaborative process which any evaluation would focus. Thus, 'rationalism—modernism emphasizes delivery of community service (outcomes for communities and clients), postmodernism stresses the internal adaptive capacity of collaboration arrangements' (ibid.: 722). Adaptive capacity has been defined as a 'dynamic process of continuous learning and adjustment that permits ambiguity and complexity' (Staber and Sydow, 2002: 410). It is viewed to consist of three core characteristics:

(i)   diversity (for instance, inclusion of relevant actors in collaborative arrangements);
(ii) opportunity for interaction (such as accessibility for repeated face-to-face dialogue); and

(iii) methods of selection (such as continuous learning to eliminate ineffective strategies, actors, outcomes).

These properties then become guiding principles for interactions between collaborative partners (see Innes and Booher, 2010; Scholz and Stiftel, 2005). However, when this hypothesis was tested in a study involving Swedish municipalities, it produced a weak corelation with service delivery but a positive corelation between goal attainment variables of different partners (Nohrstedt, 2015: 729–730). This finding is contrary to evidence from other studies examining corelation between the number of partners and collaboration performance (Kerslake Inquiry, 2018; Turrini et al., 2010). Additionally, the multi-centric nature of such collaborations increases the potential risks due to the diversity of partners, the nature of risk itself and the complexity in managing the project. Carr and Hawkins (2013), in their study on service collaborations in the U.S., identify various types of risk arising due to coordination, division, and defection costs and suggest measures to reduce or minimise such risks through the use of specific contracts and different institutional arrangements.

Evidence in relation to 'routine' management of emergencies by collaborative partners is equally inconclusive or sparse (Parry et al., 2015; Pitts, 2008; Pollock, 2013). A study looking at a range of factors and outcomes of collaborative response to severe winter conditions in Sweden showed that prior experience of hazard is unrelated to involvement in collaborative activity and found no relationship between perceived problem severity or number of partners and outcomes at network and community level (see Nohrstedt, 2016, for a fuller discussion). These findings are in conflict with previous studies reported elsewhere (see Nohrstedt, 2015; McGuire and Silvia, 2010). The need for further research and empirical studies to test adaptive capacity in collaborative projects and its impact on service delivery, both in routine emergencies or serious events, clearly follows from this analysis.

Theoretical framework(s) to explain emergency collaboration

The provision of police, ambulance, and fire services are among the core largest tasks for local governments. Public spending on the three emergency services in the U.K. was close to £21 billion in 2020/2021 (Clark, 2021; NAO, 2017). The U.S. local governments spent $112 billion on police and fire services in 2021, second only to education spending of $126 billion (Barnett et al., 2014). However, many of these services across the western hemisphere have experienced budget cuts and some of these cuts are ongoing leading to layoffs, redundancies, hiring freezes, or even abolition of departments or services (Wilson and Grammich, 2015). This has also led to emergence of new models of service delivery, contracting out or sharing resources and manpower to achieve efficiency and cost-effectiveness (Parry et al., 2015; Chermak et al., 2014; Charman, 2019; Murphy et al., 2019).

As indicated earlier in this chapter, a plethora of models/approaches exist and are practiced around the world. Consolidation of the ambulance, police, and the fire services has taken the form of a 'public-safety' agency in the U.S. with over 130 such agencies now established by the local municipalities (Wilson and Grammich, 2015). In the U.K., the police and fire services have been placed under the single administrative department (Home Office) since 2017. Legislative and policy changes in 2017 have led to a joint governance of the police and fire services by the Police and Crime Commissioners (PCCs) in six cases by March 2022 (this includes the two mayors who are also PFCCs) and creation of a new joint inspection regime for the police and fire services (HMICFRS, 2019). In Scotland, a national model of a single police service (after merger of eight respective regional forces in 2013) and fire service (after merger of eight local services and the national training agency) and single ambulance service (since 1995) exists. Wales also has a national ambulance service, four police and three fire services.

The literature also highlights the 'partnership' continuums or ranges developed from practice in the noughties. Figure 3.1, adapted from Wilson

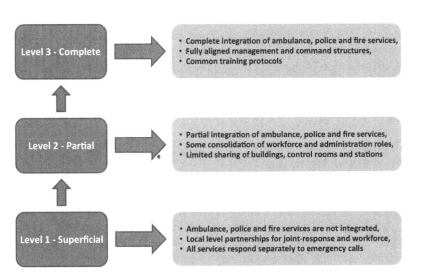

Figure 3.1 Levels of integration between emergency services

(adapted from Wilson and Grammich, 2015: 363)

and Grammich (2015), depicts the levels of integration available to emergency services. A complete integration would entail creation of a single entity with cross-trained staff to deliver the police, ambulance and fire services. The U.S. experiment with the 'public-safety' agencies, discussed earlier, would fall into such a category wherein the police and fire services are jointly delivered. Partial integration entails limited consolidation of the three services. Cross-trained staff represent the three services separately while working together. The U.K. PCC experiment of joint governance of the fire and police services falls under this category. The third category of superficial integration doesn't entail any meaningful consolidation while still sharing resources such as office/staff buildings, control rooms, stations, or vehicles. They still represent their individual departments. Such collaborations are quite common at local level addressing specific issues and the three emergency services routinely respond collaboratively during major incidents or dealing with specific threats. It is also worth noting that most collaborations would fall somewhere on this continuum across the three levels but these positions could very well shift since there are a range of factors that come into play in determining or sustaining the level and nature of any collaboration.

The desire for collaborations and the institutional, policy and legislative drivers can vary significantly, making an objective evaluation of such collaborations significantly more difficult, especially in a short term (Bryson et al., 2015). In their analysis of six public-safety agencies in the U.S., Wilson and Grammich (2015: 374) found evidence for 'structural contingency and institutional variation in organizational structures and agency practice' which helped to explain factors favouring consolidation (integration) or deconsolidation in the agencies explored. In a comprehensive evaluation of the emergency services collaborations carried out on behalf of the U.K. government, Parry et al. (2015) made wide ranging suggestions on three key aspects namely;

(i)   increasing collaboration;
(ii)   removing barriers; and
(iii) promoting enablers.

Adopting a rigorous methodology involving interviews, focus groups and surveys with emergency services staff and leaders, they reported their findings by splitting them into three levels of support (substantial, strong, and mixed). See Table 3.3 for a summary of these recommendations.

This evidence suggests that collaborations are driven by reasons of both efficiency and effectiveness and the need to save money. However, they are also about delivering better services and improving societal outcomes.

Table 3.3 Summary of recommendations for effective collaborations

Level 1: characterised by substantial support and deliverability	• The creation of more single back offices • Adoption of shared key performance indicators • Further capital resource rationalisation • Adoption of co-located control rooms • More funding streams • Promotion of good practise • Sharing of individual service data • Further implementation of common protocols
Level 2: characterised by strong support but with more issues to manage/overcome	• Implementation of shared operational staff • Development of shared command structures • Address the disparity in data collection • Increase in joint training programmes • Supporting leadership • More direction from central government
Level 3: characterised by mixed support and with key barriers to manage/overcome	• More integrated local and national governance structures • The adoption of integrated control rooms • The adoption of one merged local budget • Alignment of terms and conditions • More comprehensive intra-service rationalisation • Police devolution

Source: Adapted from Parry et al. (2015: 36)

The sustainability of collaborations is also linked to consistent messaging across government departments, local decisions about future direction and political will and non-partisan support and endorsement (Parry et al., 2015; Wilson and Grammich, 2015; Wegner and Verschoore, 2022). Wankhade and Patnaik (2019: 7) have argued that successful collaborations are dependent on separate but inter-connected elements of people, processes, systems, and technology and a 'one size fits all' is likely to fail given the variability of emergency services provision.

This discussion highlights several challenges and pitfalls in trying to identify a unified theory for emergency services collaboration and/or whether the ideal corresponds with the reality of emergency or crisis management (Nohrstedt, 2013). The situation is best summed up by Rosenthal et al. (1991: 212–213), who argue:

'there is little evidence of the validity of the continuing normative assumption of overriding consensus, unanimity, and solidarity amongst actors and agencies involved in managing crisis events.'

This makes the subject fascinating to research but difficult for scholars and practitioners to find appropriate evidence and support. Nevertheless, researchers have attempted to use different theoretical lenses to make sense of this phenomenon. Nohrstedt (2013: 965) has argued that the potentially (adversarial) nature of crisis resolution calls for better integration and links between emergency and crisis management literature and public policy theory. Weible et al. (2008) have presented the Advocacy Coalition Framework (ACF) as a possible public policy analytical tool to map political conflict in crisis resolution, Nohrstedt (2013) applies the ACF to analyse the European response and stakeholder conflict in relation to the volcanic ash cloud crisis of 2010. Briefly, ACF provides a set of five broad assumptions that are designed to guide the analysis of policy conflict in crisis situations and were found to be useful in EU-related problems (Radaelli, 1999; Nedergaard, 2008; Weible, 2008). These include:

(i)   policy subsystems as unit of analysis;
(ii)   the role of scientific information;
(iii) competing case narratives;
(iv)   mobilisation of political resources and policy venues; and
(v)   opportunities and policy change.

However, the ACF is not free from limitations and the stable subsystem relationships and interactions posited by ACF may not be suitable for analysing a shorter episode or an unfolding crisis like a terrorist attack (Nohrstedt, 2013). Further research to test the suitability of ACF in understanding the complexities in a variety of crisis resolution situations and contexts is also supported by the proponents of the approach (Weible et al., 2011).

Elements of structural contingency and institutional theories have also been applied to the study of public-safety agencies in the U.S. (Wilson and Grammich, 2015). According to structural contingency theory, size, age, nature of tasks, and the environment in which an organisation is embedded determine its structure and activities and the contingencies are the events or characteristics that are mutually dependent (Wilson and Grammich, 2015). Hence organisations seek to fit 'their structure to the task contingency in order to yield operational and managerial effectiveness' (Donaldson, 1995: 27). This could be done by way of an increase in the 'degree of bureaucratisation' as it increases size or by way of altering their structure to reduce misfit and restore equilibrium. Wilson and Grimmich (2015) argue that as per contingency theory, 'municipalities may implement public-safety consolidation to the extent it helps them effectively provide police and fire services to their community (i.e. maximizes performance)—and abandon it when the structure no longer fits their communities' (p. 364). The study reported both contingency and institutional variations in decisions by the chosen agencies to either consolidate or deconsolidate. Wider application of the study findings is limited by its case study method, but it helps frame questions for organisations seeking integration (see also Weinholt and Andersson Granberg, 2015).

Conclusion

Existing studies on individual blue light organisations sensitise us to deeply held cultural values amongst organisational members (see Wankhade et al., 2018; Chan, 1997). We have argued elsewhere (Wankhade and Patnaik, 2019) that the success of collaborations amongst blue light organisations is not simply about why and under what institutional condition they are formed, rather how each collaboration is managed, evaluated, and sustained over time. Successful collaborations are also contingent upon rigorous assessment of challenges and engagement by stakeholders and require a clear rationale for collaboration which goes beyond efficiency and the need to save money argument but is also driven by improving service delivery and outcomes for different stakeholders (Chen, 2010; Kane, 2018; Parry et al., 2015).

The next chapter explores the issues of leadership and culture in emergency services.

References

Adams, I., and Mastracci, S. (2019). Police body-worn cameras: Effects on officers' burnout and perceived organizational support. *Police Quarterly*, 22(1): 5–30.

Agrawal, M. (2003). Impact of mobile computing terminals in police work. *Journal of Organizational Computing and Electronic Commerce*, 13(2): 73–89.

Balcik, B., Beamon, B., Krejci, C., Muramatsu, K., and Ramirez, M. (2010). Coordination in humanitarian relief chains: Practices, challenges and opportunities. *International Journal of Production Economics*, 126(1): 22–34.

Barnett, J.L., Sheckells, C.L., Peterson, S., and Tydings, E.M. (2014). *2012 Census of Governments: Finance—State and Local Government Summary Report.* U.S. Census Bureau, Economy-Wide Statistics Briefs: Public Sector. Retrieved from: http://www2.census.gov/govs/local/summary_report.pdf.

Barraket, J., McNeill, J., Campbell, P., and Carey, G. (2021). Navigating network governance: The role of social enterprise in local employment services. *Public Management Review*, 1–22.

Bea, K. (2005). *Emergency Management Preparedness Standards: Overview and Options for Congress.* Ft. Belfoir Defense Technical Information Centre. Report No: CRS-RL32520. Corp and Library of Congress. Washington, DC: Congressional Research Service.

Blomgren Bingham, L., O'Leary, R., and Carlson, C. (2008). Frameshifting: Lateral thinking for collaborative public management. In L. Blomgren Bingham and R. O'Leary (eds.), *Big Ideas in Collaborative Public Management*, 3–35. Armonk, NY: M.E. Sharpe.

Bodin, Ö. (2017). Collaborative environmental governance: Achieving collective action in social-ecological systems. *Science*, 357(6352): eaan1114. https://doi. org/10.1126/science.aan1114

Boin, A., and 't Hart, P. (2010). Organizing for effective emergency management: Lessons from research. *Australian Journal of Public Administration*, 69(4): 357–371.

Bolda, E.J., Saucier, P., Maddox, G.L., Wetle, T., and Lowe, J.I. (2006). Governance and management structures for community partnerships: Experiences from the robert wood johnson foundation's community partnerships for older adults program. *The Gerontologist*, 46: 391–397.

Brunetto, Y., Farr-Wharton, B., Wankhade, P., Saccon, C., and Xerri, M. (2022). Managing emotional labour: The importance of organisational support for managing police officers in England and Italy (forthcoming). *The International Journal of Human Resource Management*. http://doi.org/10.1080/09585192.2022.2047755

Bryson, J.M., Crosby, B.C., and Middleton, S.M. (2006). The design and implementation of cross-sector collaborations: Propositions from the literature. *Public Administration Review*, 66: 44–55.

Bryson, J.M., Crosby, B.C., and Stone, M.M. (2015). Designing and implementing cross sector collaborations: Needed and challenging. *Public Administration Review*, 75: 647–663.

Cabinet Office. (2013). *The Role of Local Resilience Forums: A Reference Document (version 2)*. London: TSO.

Carr , J.B., and Hawkins, C.V. (2013). The costs of cooperation: What the research tells us about managing the risks of service collaborations in the U.S. *State and Local Government Review*, 45(4): 224–239.

Chan, J. B. L. (1997). *Changing Police Culture*. Cambridge: Cambridge University Press.

Charman, S. (2017). *Police Socialisation, Identity and Culture: Becoming Blue*. Basingstoke: Palgrave.

Charman, S. (2019). Changing landscapes, changing identities – Policing in England and Wales. In P. Wankhade, L. McCann, and P. Murphy (eds.), *Critical Perspectives on the Management and Organization of Emergency Services*. Abingdon: Routledge.

Chen, B. (2010). Antecedents or processes? Determinants of perceived effectiveness of interorganizational collaborations for public service delivery. *International Public Management Journal*, 13(4): 381–407.

Chermak, S., Scheer, C., and Wilson, J.M. (2014). Police consolidation in the news. *Police Quarterly*, 17(6): 150–175.

Clark, D. (2021). Public sector expenditure on the police service in the United Kingdom from 2009/10 to 2020/21. *Statistica*. Available at: www.statista.com/statistics/298637/united-kingdom-uk-public-sector-expenditure-police-services/

Comfort, L.K. (2007). Crisis management in hindsight: Cognition, communication, coordination, and control. *Public Administration Review*, 67: 189–197.

Crosby, B.C., and Bryson, J.M. (2018). Why leadership of public leadership research matters: And what to do about it? *Public Management Review*, 20(9): 1265–1286.

Diehlmann, F., Lüttenberg, M., Verdonck, L., Wiens, M., Zienau, A., and Schultmann, F. (2021). Public-private collaborations in emergency logistics: A framework based on logistical and game-theoretical concepts. *Safety Science*, 141: 105301.

Donaldson, L. (1995). *American Anti-Management Theories of Organization: A Critique of Paradigm Proliferation*. Cambridge: Cambridge University Press.

Eide, W.A., Haugstveit, I.M., Halvorsrud, R., Skjetne, J.H., and Stiso, M. (2012). *Key Challenges in Multi-agency Collaboration During Large-Scale Emergency Management. In AmI for Crisis Management, International Joint Conference on Ambient Intelligence*. Italy: Pisa.

El Ansari, W., and Weiss, E.S. (2006). Quality of re-search on community partnerships: Developing the evidence base. *Health and Education Re-search: Theory and Practice*, 21: 175–180.

Foster-Fishman, P.G., Berkopwitz, S.L., Louns-bury, D.W., Jacobson, S., and Allen, N.A. (2001). Building collaborative capacity in community coalitions: A review and integrative framework. *American Journal of Community Psychology*, 29: 241–261.

Gabler, C.B., Richey, R.G., and Stewart, G.T. (2017). Disaster resilience through public-private short-term collaboration. *Journal of Business Logistics*, 38(2): 130–144.

Grenfell Inquiry Report. (2019). *Grenfell Tower Inquiry Phase 1 Report of the Public Inquiry into the Fire at Grenfell Tower on 14 June 2017*. Available at: https://www.grenfelltowerinquiry.org.uk/phase-1-report.

Grimshaw, D., Vincent, S., and Willmott, H. (2002). Going privately: Partnership and outsourcing in UK public services. *Public Administration*, 80(3): 475–502.

Hedlund, J., Bodin, O., and Nohrstedt, D. (2020). Policy issue interdependency and the formation of collaborative networks. *People and Nature*, 3(1): 236–250.

Her Majesty's Inspectorate of Constabulary and Fire & Rescue Services HMICFRS. (2017). *Proposed Fire and Rescue Services Inspection Programme and Framework 2018/19*. Available at: https://www.justiceinspectorates.gov.uk/hmicfrs/publications/frs-inspection-programme-consultation-2018-19/ [Accessed 10 November 2022].

Her Majesty's Inspectorate of Constabulary and Fire & Rescue Services HMICFRS. (2019). *Fire and Rescue Service Assessments*. Available at: https://www.justiceinspectorates.gov.uk/hmicfrs/frs-assessment/frs-2018/ [Accessed 10 October 2022].

Hesselman, M., and Lane, L. (2017). Disasters and non-state actors—human rights-based approaches. *Disaster Prevention and Management: An International Journal*, 26(5): 526–539.

Hicklin, A., O'Toole, L.J., Jr., Meier, K.J., and Robinson, S.E. (2009). Calming the storms: Collaborative public management, hurricanes Katrina, Rita, and disaster response. In R. O'Leary and L.B. Bingham (eds.), *The Collaborative Public Manager*, 95–114. Washington, DC: Georgetown University Press.

Horwitz, S. (2009). Walmart to the rescue: Private enterprise's response to Hurricane Katrina. *The Independent Review*, 13(4): 511–528.

Huxham, C. (2000). The challenge of collaborative governance. *Public Management*, 2: 337–357.

Huxham, C., and Vangen, C. (2005). *Managing to Collaborate: The Theory and Practice of Collaborative Advantage*. New York: Routledge

Innes, J., and Booher, D. (2010). *Planning with Complexity: An Introduction to Collaborative Rationality for Public Policy*. New York: Routledge.

Izumi, T., and Shaw, R. (2015). Overview and introduction of the private sector's role in disaster management. In T. Izumi and R. Shaw (eds.), *Disaster Management and Private Sectors: Challenges and Potentials*, 1–10. Tokyo: Springer.

Jones, C., Hesterly, W., and Borgatti, S. (1997). A general theory of network governance: Ex-change conditions and social mechanisms. *The Academy of Management Review*, 22(4): 911–945.

Jones, N., and Thomas, P. (2007). Inter-organizational collaboration and partnerships in health and social care: The role of social software. *Public Policy and Administration*, 22: 289–302.

Kale, P., and Singh, H. (2009). Managing strategic alliances: What do we know now, and where do we go from here? *Academy of Management Perspectives*, 23(3): 45–62.

Kane, E. (2018). Collaboration in the emergency services. In P. Murphy and K. Greenhalgh (eds.), *Fire and Rescue Services: Leadership and Management Perspectives*, 77–91. Geneva: Springer.

Kapucu, N. (2005). Interorganizational coordination in dynamic context: Networks in emergency response management. *Connections*, 26(2): 33–48.

Kapucu, N. (2008). Collaborative emergency management: Better community organising, better public preparedness and response. *Disasters*, 32: 239–262.

Kapucu, N., and Van Wart, M. (2006). The evolving role of the public sector in managing catastrophic disasters: Lessons learned. *Administration & Society*, 38: 279–308.

Kapucu, N., Arslan, T., and Collins, M. (2010). Examining intergovernmental and interorganizational response to catastrophic disasters: Toward a network-centric approach. *Administration & Society*, 42: 222–247.

Kapucu, N., Augustin, M.E., and Garayev, V. (2009). Interstate partnerships in emergency management: Emergency management assistance compact in response to catastrophic disasters. *Public Administration Review*, 69: 297–313.

Kelman, S., Hong, S., and Turbitt, I. (2013) . Are there managerial practices associated with the outcomes of an interagency service delivery collaboration? Evidence from British crime and disorder reduction partnerships. *Journal of Public Administration Research and Theory*, 23(3): 609–630.

Kerka, S. (1997). Developing collaborative partner-ships. In *Practice Application Brief*. Columbus, OH: Center on Education and Training for Employment, Ohio State University.

Kerslake Report. (2018). *An Independent Review Into the Preparedness for, and Emergency Response to, the Manchester Arena Attack on 22nd May 2017*. https://www.kerslakearenareview.co.uk/media/1022/kerslake_arena_review_printed_final.pdf

Langford, J. (2002). Managing public-private partnerships in Canada. In M. Edwards and J. Langford (eds.), *New Players, Partners and Processes: A Public Sector Without Boundaries*. Canberra: National Institute for Governance and Centre for Public Sector Studies, 68–84.

Latour, B. (1991). Technology is society made durable. In J. Law (ed.), *A Sociology of Monsters: Essays on Power, Technology and Domination*, 103–131. London: Routledge.

Loftus, B.(2009). *Police Culture in a Changing World*. Oxford: Oxford University Press.

Lubell, M. (2013). Governing institutional complexity: The ecology of games framework. *Policy Studies Journal*, 41(3): 537–560.

Lyon, D. (2003). *Surveillance After September 11*. Cambridge: Polity Press.

Maguire, E.R. (2003). *Organizational Structure in American Police Agencies: Context, Complexity, and Control*. Albany: State University of New York Press.

Mandell, M., and Keast, R. (2008). Evaluating network arrangements: Toward revised performance measures. *Public Performance and Management Review*, 30(4): 574–597.

Manning, P. (2008). *The Technology of Policing: Crime Mapping, Information Technology, and the Rationality of Crime Control*. New York: New York University Press.

Martin, N., Verdonck, L., Caris, A., and Depaire, B. (2018). Horizontal collaboration in logistics: Decision framework and typology. *Operations Management Research*, 11(1–2): 32–50.

McCann, L., and Granter, E. (2019). Beyond 'blue-collar professionalism': Continuity and change in the professionalization of uniformed emergency services work. *Journal of Professions and Organizations*, 6(3): 213–232.

McGuire, M., and Silvia, C. (2010). The effect of problem severity, managerial and organizational capacity, and agency structure on intergovernmental collaboration: Evidence from local emergency management. *Public Administration Review*, 70: 279–288.

Meurs, T., and Noordegraaf, M. (2022). Adapted agency: How connected (Dutch) police professionals rework their professional capabilities. *Journal of Professions and Organization*, 19.

Meyer, J.W., and Rowan, B. (1977). Institutionalized organizations: Formal structure as myth and ceremony. *American Journal of Sociology*, 83: 340–363.

Murphy, P. (2006). *Intelligence and Security Committee: Report into the London Terrorist Attacks on 7 July 2005*. London: HM Stationery Office, Cm 6785.

Murphy, P., Ferry, L., Glennon, R., and Greenhalgh, K. (2019). *Public Service Accountability: Rekindling a Debate*. Cham, Switzerland: Palgrave Macmillan.

Murphy, P., Wankhade, P., and Lakoma, K. (2020). The strategic and operational landscape of emergency services in the UK. *International Journal of Emergency Services*, 9(1): 69–88.

National Audit Office. (2017). *NHS Ambulance Services*. London: National Audit Office.

National Commission on Terrorist Attacks upon the United States. (2004). *The 9/11 Commission Report: Final Report of the National Commission on Terrorist Attacks Upon the United States*. New York: W.W. Norton.

Nedergaard, P. (2008). The reform of the 2003 common agricultural policy: An advocacy coalition explanation. *Policy Studies*, 29(2): 179–195.

Newig, J., Challies, E.D., Jager, N.W., Kochskaemper, E., and Adzersen, A. (2018). The environmental performance of participatory and collaborative governance: A framework of causal mechanisms. *Policy Studies Journal*, 46(2): 269–297.

Niesten, E., and Jolink, A. (2015). Alliance management capabilities and performance. *International Journal of Management Reviews*, 17: 69–100.

Nohrstedt, D. (2013). Advocacy coalitions in crisis resolution: Understanding policy dispute in the European volcanic ash cloud crisis. *Public Administration*, 91(4): 964–979.

Nohrstedt, D. (2015). Does adaptive capacity influence service delivery? Evidence from Swedish emergency management collaborations. *Public Management Review*, 17(5): 718–735.

Nohrstedt, D. (2015). Does adaptive capacity influence service delivery? Evidence from Swedish emergency management collaborations. *Public Management Review*, 17(5): 718–735.

Nohrstedt, D. (2016). Explaining mobilization and performance of collaborations in routine emergency management. *Administration & Society*, 48(2): 135–162.

Palen, L., Vieweg, S., Liu, S., and Hughes, A.L. (2009). Crisis in a networked world. Features of computer mediated communication in the April 16, 2007, Virginia Tech Event. *Social Science Computer Review*, 27(4): 467–480.

Papadopoulos, T., Gunasekaran, A., Dubey, R., Altay, N., Childe, S.J., and Fosso-Wamba, S. (2017). The role of big data in explaining disaster resilience in supply chains for sustainability. *Journal of Cleaner Production*, 142: 1108–1118.

Parry, J., Kane, E., Martin, D., and Bandyopadhyay, S. (2015). *Research Into Emergency Services Collaboration*. Emergency Services Working Group Research Project. Sheffield University.

Peters, B.G. (1996). *The Future of Governing: Four Emerging Models*. Lawrence: University of Kansas Press.

Peters, B.G. (1998). Managing horizontal government: The politics of co-ordination. *Public Administration*, 76: 295–311.

Peters, B.G. (2015). *Advanced Introduction to Public Policy*. Cheltenham, UK: Edward Elgar.

Pitt, M. (2008). *Lessons Learned From the 2007 Floods*. London: Cabinet Office.

Pollitt, C., and Bouckaert, G. (2017). *Public Management Reform: A Comparative Analysis—Into the Age of Austerity*. Oxford: Oxford University Press.

Pollock, K. (2013). *Review of Persistent Lessons Identified Relating to Interoperability From Emergencies and Major Incidents Since 1986. A Report Commissioned by the Cabinet Office Civil Contingencies Secretariat*. Available at: https://jesip.org.uk/uploads/media/Documents%20Products/Pollock_Review_Oct_2013.pdf [Accessed 20 July 2018].

Prosser, T., and Taylor, M. (2020). *The Grenfell Tower Fire: Benign Neglect and the Road to an Avoidable Tragedy*. Shoreham-by-Sea: Pavilion.

Radaelli, C. (1999). Harmful tax competition in the EU: Policy narratives and advocacy coalitions. *Journal of Common Market Studies*, 37(4): 661–682.

Ready, J.T., and Young, J.T.N. (2015). The impact of on-officer video cameras on police—citizen contacts: Findings from a controlled experiment in Mesa, AZ. *Journal of Experimental Criminology*, 11: 445–458.

Reid, R., and Jowell, T. (2006). *Addressing Lessons from the Emergency Response to the 7 July 2005 London Bombings: What We Learned and What We Are Doing about It*. London: Stationery Office.

Robinson, S., and Gaddis, B. (2012) Seeing past parallel play: Survey measures of collaboration in disaster situations. *Policy Studies Journal*, 40(2): 256–273.

Rosenthal, U., 't Hart, P., and Kouzmin, A. (1991). The bureau-politics of crisis management. *Public Administration*, 69(2): 211–233.

Sanders, C.B. (2014). Need to know vs. need to share: Information technology and the intersecting work of police, fire and paramedics. *Information, Communication & Society*, 17(4): 463–475.

Scholz, J., and Stiftel, B. (2005). *Adaptive Governance and Water Conflict*. Washington, DC: RFF Press.

Scottish Government. (2012). *Preparing Scotland: Scottish Guidance on Resilience: Philosophy, Principles, Structures, Regulatory Duties*. Edinburgh: Scottish Government.

Sparf, J., and Petridoua, E. (2018). Collaborations in routine emergency management: Lessons from Sweden. *Procedia Engineering*, 212: 302–308.

Staber, U., and Sydow, B. (2002). Organizational adaptive capacity: A structuration perspective. *Journal of Management Inquiry*, 11(4): 408–424.

Storm, K.J., and Eyerman, J. (2006). Interagency coordination: Lessons learned from the 2005 London train bombings. *NIJ Journal*, 261: 28–32.

Suchman, L. (1987). *Plans and Situated Actions*. Cambridge: Cambridge University Press.

Szirom, T., Hyde, J., Lasater, Z., and Moore, C. (2002). *Working Together – Integrated Governance*. Brisbane: Institute of Public Administration, Australia.

Todak, N., Gaub, J.E., and White, M.D. (2018). The importance of external stakeholders for police body-worn camera diffusion. *Policing: An International Journal*, 41(4): 448–464.

Todeva, E., and Knoke, D. (2005). Strategic alliance sand models of collaboration. *Management Decision*, 43: 123–148.

Turrini, A., Christofoli, D., Fosini, F., and Nasi, G. (2010). Networking literature about determinants of network effectiveness. *Public Administration*, 88: 528–550.

US Government Printing Office. (2006). Hurricane Katrina: A nation still unprepared. *Special Report of the Committee on Homeland Security and Governmental Affairs United States Senate. 109th Congress*. 2nd Session, SPECIAL REPORT S. Rept. 109–322. Available at: www.govinfo.gov/content/pkg/CRPT-109srpt322/pdf/CRPT-109srpt322.pdf

Van Wassenhove, L. (2006). Humanitarian aid logistics: Supply chain management in high gear. *Journal of the Operational Research Society*, 57(5): 475–489.

Vangen, S., and Huxham, C. (2012). The tangled web: Unravelling the principle of common goals in collaborations. *Journal of Public Administration Research and Theory*, 22(4): 731–760.

Vangen, S., Hayes, J.P., and Cornforth, C. (2015). Governing cross-sector interorganizational collaborations. *Public Management Review*, 17(9): 1237–1260.

Vanneste, B.S. (2016). From interpersonal to interorganisational trust: The role of indirect reciprocity. *Journal of Trust Research*, 6(1): 7–36.

Verdonck, L. (2017). *Collaborative Logistics From the Perspective of Freight Transport Companies*. PhD thesis. University of Hasselt, Diepenbeek, Belgium.

Verstrepen, S., Cools, M., Cruijssen, F., and Dullaert, W. (2009). A dynamic framework for managing horizontal cooperation in logistics. *International Journal of Logistics Systems and Management*, 5(3–4): 228–248.

Wang, X., and Kopfer, H. (2011)2. Increasing efficiency of freight carriers through collaborative transport planning: Chances and challenges. In *Proceedings of the Sixth German Russian Logistics and SCM Workshop* (DR-LOG 2011), pp. 1–010. http://www.sfb637.uni-bremen.de/pubdb/repository/SFB637-B9-11-005-IC.pdf

Wankhade, P. (2012). Different cultures of management and their relationships with organisational performance: Evidence from the UK ambulance service. *Public Money & Management*, 32(5): 381–388.

Wankhade, P., and Murphy, P. (2012). Bridging the theory and practice gap in emergency services research: Case for a new journal. *International Journal of Emergency Services*, 1(1): 4–9.

Wankhade, P., and Patnaik, S. (2019). *Collaboration and Governance in the Emergency Services: Issues, Opportunities and Challenges*. London: Palgrave Macmillan.

Wankhade, P., Heath, G., and Radcliffe, J. (2018). Cultural change and perpetuation in organisations: Evidence from an English emergency ambulance service. *Public Management Review*, 20(6): 923–948.

Wankhade, P., McCann, L., and Murphy, P. (eds.). (2019). *Critical Perspectives on the Management and Organization of Emergency Services*. New York: Routledge.

Wankhade, P., Stokes, P., Tarba, S., and Rodgers, P. (2020). Work intensification and ambidexterity—the notions of extreme and 'everyday' experiences in emergency contexts: Surfacing dynamics in the ambulance service. *Public Management Review*, 22(1): 48–74.

Warburton, J., and Petriwskyj, A.M. (2007). Older but involved: Community partnerships in the development of ageing policies in Australia. *Just Policy*, 45: 38–44.

Warburton, J., Everingham, J.-A., Cuthill, M., and Bartlett, H. (2008). Achieving effective collaborations to help communities age well. *The Australian Journal of Public Administration*, 67(4): 470–482.

Waugh, W.L. (2003). Terrorism, homeland security, and the national emergency management network. *Public Organization Review*, 3: 373–385.

Wegner, D., and Verschoore, J. (2022). Network governance in action: Functions and practices to foster collaborative environments. *Administration & Society*, 54(3): 479–499.

Weible, C. (2008). Expert-based information and policy subsystems: A review and synthesis. *Policy Studies Journal*, 36(4): 615–635.

Weible, C., Sabatier, P., and Flowers, J. (2008). The advocacy coalition framework. In *Encyclopedia of Public Administration and Public Policy*, 2nd ed., 1, 1, 1–10. New York: Routledge.

Weible, C., Sabatier, P., Jenkins-Smith, H., Nohrstedt, D., Henry, A., and DeLeon, P. (2011). A quarter century of the advocacy coalition framework: An introduction to the special issue. *Policy Studies Journal*, 39(3): 349–360.

Weinholt, Å., and Andersson Granberg, T. (2015). New collaborations in daily emergency response: Applying cost-benefit analysis to new first response initiatives in the Swedish fire and rescue service. *International Journal of Emergency Services*, 4(2): 177–193.

Weinholt, Å., and Andersson Granberg, T. (2015). New collaborations in daily emergency response: Applying cost-benefit analysis to new first response initiatives in the Swedish fire and rescue service. *International Journal of Emergency Services*, 4(2): 177–193.

Wilson, J.M., and Grammich, C.A. (2015). Deconsolidation of public- safety agencies providing police and fire services. *International Criminal Justice Review*, 25(4): 361–378.

Zaré, M., and Afrouz, S.G. (2012). Crisis management of tohoku: Japan earthquake and tsunami, 11 March 2011. *Iranian Journal of Public Health*, 41(6): 12–20.

4 Leadership and culture(s)
Still command and control?

Introduction

Call for effective leadership in organisations is a constant theme of management inquiry. Good leaders and effective leadership are seen as a 'sine qua non' of a successful organisation and for meeting the ostensibly endless process of societal and business upheaval. The emergency services have not been immune from such changes. Rising demand for services, shrinking public budgets, out-sourcing, downsizing and performance management are some of the issues which most emergency services personnel have encountered at various points in time and have been well documented in the literature (Wankhade and Patnaik, 2019; McCann and Granter, 2019; Yates, 1999). Such challenges inevitably bring additional and new demands on emergency services leadership to cope with such issues and find a solution, further putting into the spotlight the leader's performance which may be critical to the functioning and sustainability of the organisation including the well-being and resilience of staff (Yates, 1999; Owen et al., 2015; Wankhade et al., 2019).

In Chapter 3, we highlighted the increasingly collaborative nature of emergency response and the challenges involved in sustaining such collaborative networks. Demands confronted by leaders today are more complex than those faced by their predecessors, requiring constant adaptation and interventions to mitigate injuries and safeguard life and property (Caro, 2016; Murphy and Dunn, 2012). Emergency services are also witnessing a significant shift in the nature, frequency and scale of disasters (both natural or man-made), and societal pressures which are often complex and occur simultaneously. Good leadership, in our view, is key to effective emergency response management and can *be* the difference between success and failure.

This chapter begins with an oversight of the current leadership structures/styles in the emergency services, highlighting the continuing influence of

DOI: 10.4324/9781003198017-4

command-and-control aspects of leadership and how it compares with contemporary leadership studies. It is followed by a brief look at the organisational culture of emergency services and calls for greater collaborative approaches to leadership and leadership development before offering some concluding remarks.

State of emergency services leadership

The three emergency services have developed historically in an *ad hoc* manner, each having a different professionalisation history, a separate road map for modernisation and future direction of travel. The multiplicity of governance and organisational models around the world, each with its unique service delivery models, performance metrics and structures coupled with a contested political and policy landscape further complicates the terrain and acts as a challenge to developing effective leadership models and styles. Historically, emergency services have been organisationally structured in a hierarchical manner with clear command and control lines of communication to support ranks and seniority (Wankhade and Brinkman, 2014). The rank and uniforms, coupled with dominant and collectively held beliefs within the organisations, encouraged social identities with clear boundaries and stereotyped 'heroic' models of leadership with little or no challenge to senior management decision making providing the opportunities for a 'blame culture' to develop (Wankhade and Patnaik, 2019; Wankhade et al., 2018; Eyre, 2018; Owen et al., 2015; Owen, 2013). This created background conditions where frontline staff and junior ranked officers do not feel confident (without reprisals) to share, challenge, or contribute to build 'collective meaning structures' (see Kruke and Olsen, 2012). This is particularly important for emergency services personnel who often deal with traumatic events and require the confidence and support of senior management to work and make critical time-sensitive decisions in a high pressure and emotionally challenging environment (Knox, 2019). The lack of support from senior leadership is crucial and unsurprisingly it has been demonstrated that '*toxic leadership behaviours*' can influence the efficiency required to operate in the complex world of emergency services (Irons, 2017: 11).

In our own work we have found a lack of critical engagement of frontline staff and managers in decision making is resulting in poor staff relations, poor wellbeing, and difficulties with staff retention and engagement (see Wankhade, 2021; Wankhade et al., 2020; Granter et al., 2019; Wankhade, 2016). Recent evidence highlights the significance of organisational support as an integral part of managing emotional labour of frontline emergency services staff and driving motivational levels (see Brunetto et al., 2022; Farr-Wharton et al., 2022; Wankhade, 2021; Purba and Demou, 2019; Cook et al., 2019).

Like any other public sector organisations which have either embraced or been subjected to New Public Management (NPM) regimes, tools and principles, emergency services are also experiencing downsizing, outsourcing, job share, job redesign, and job-freeze (McCann and Granter, 2019; Murphy et al., 2020). NPM and the tight fiscal climate are also resulting into a more flatter or reduced middle managerial roles for allegedly more efficient structures. The separation of junior and frontline officers located in dispersed stations with senior leadership at headquarters can result in communication gaps and potential dis-enchantment and disengagement across organisations which have had adverse implications during crisis such as Manchester Arena Attack or the Grenfell Fire tragedy in 2017 (see Kerslake Inquiry, 2018; Grenfell Inquiry Report, 2019; Saunders, 2022).

Leadership research in extreme contexts and settings has been identified as one of the least research fields in leadership research (Barton and Kahn, 2019; Barton et al., 2015; Hannah et al., 2009; Knox, 2019; Sorokin, 1943) along with being characterised as 'homogenous' (Bass, 2008, 1998). Reviewing the literature, Porter and McLaughlin (2006: 573) identified 'lack of research' on the impact of organisational context on leadership (see also Wansink et al., 2008). However, there is a growing body of work that has argued it to be uniquely contextualised and leadership function is guided by the context, including many such 'extreme contexts' (such as police, fire, military, and ambulance services) where 'risk of severe physical, psychological or material consequences to organisational members or their constituents exist' (Hannah et al., 2009: 897; see also Waugh and Streib, 2006; Fisher and Robbins, 2015; Tomkins et al., 2020; Uitdewilligen and Waller, 2018; Burke et al., 2018; Schmutz et al., 2018; Avolio et al., 2022).

Hannah et al. (2009) provide a model to understand the function of leadership in dealing with extreme events and contexts. While a more detailed analysis of the model is beyond the scope of this discussion, a brief overview is provided since it's one of the few conceptualisations available to understand how leadership works in the context of extreme events and contexts and is quoted in almost all the subsequent literature. The model details five dimensions of extreme contexts namely: time scale of events, magnitude and probability of consequences, physical, psychological, or social proximity and the form of threat. The 'level of extremity' can reduce the ability for adaptive leadership response but there are also some other factors such as organisational resources that can serve to either 'attenuate or intensify' the level of extremity experienced (see Figure 4.1).

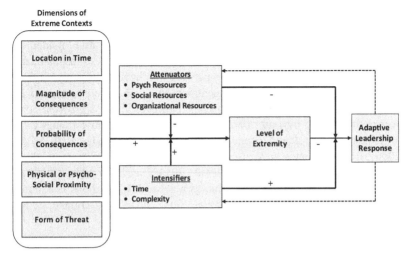

Figure 4.1 Typology of extreme contexts

Source: Hannah et al. (2009: 899). This article was published in publication titled *The Leadership Quarterly*, Vol. 20, Number 6, Hannah, S.T., Uhl-Bien, M., Avolio, B.J. and Cavarretta, F.L. A framework for examining leadership in extreme contexts, 897–919. Copyright Elsevier (2009).

The key construct in the model is that the leaders can potentially influence many of the attenuating and intensifying factors and a definition of leadership in extreme contexts is then suggested:

> Adaptive and administrative processes of influencing others to understand and agree about what needs to be done and how to do it, and the process of facilitating individual and collective efforts to accomplish shared objectives and purpose under conditions where an extensive and intolerable magnitude of physical, psychological, or material consequences may exceed an organization's capacity to counter and occur to or in close physical, social, cultural, or psychological proximity to organization members.
>
> (Hannah et al., 2009: 913)

This helps us to appreciate the contextual relevance of the disaster and the critical importance of the collaborative aspect of leadership function while dealing with extreme contexts and events. This brings us to the question of what are the leadership behaviours and model(s) which are likely to be effective in a vastly complicated, unstable, and dynamic world of extreme contexts that often face the emergency services. While we acknowledge that leadership as a concept which defies consensus: both in definition and measurement the preceding discussion highlighted some of the leadership challenges in the context of extreme events and contexts. We are reminded of Stogdill's (1974: 22) often quoted statement that 'there are almost as many definitions of leadership as there are persons who have attempted to define the concept'. Dinh et al. (2014) identified about 66 different theoretical domains and methodological approaches. However, there is growing consensus for moving beyond traditional heroic or leader-centric frameworks to a much broader shared, connected leadership capacity (Day et al., 2014, 2006). Recent debates have argued a case for a multi-level framework, a strong focus on collective (Dionne et al., 2014; Day, 2001). The notion of 'pluralised and distributed' leadership as a network of relations is gaining popularity (Bolden et al., 2008; Gronn, 2002; Dionne and Dionne, 2008; Crosby and Bryson, 2005, 2010, 2018).

Analysing the professional models used by three emergency services provides for an interesting contrast if one takes the U.K. as an illustration. The Healthcare Leadership Model (NHS, 2013) used by the ambulance services is made up of nine 'leadership dimensions' ranging from leading with care, engaging with the team and so on. But what is at the core is the idea of 'inspiring shared purpose': that leaders create a shared purpose for diverse individuals doing different work, inspiring them to believe in shared values so that they deliver benefits for patients, their families, and the community (see Figure 4.2):

The College of Policing Leadership Review (2015, 2017) concluded that no single leadership style or model can be said to be the complete answer to future demands and a collective style of leadership is found in many successful organisations. It is a style that places the leader in the role of an enabler, ultimately working to support the team. A more collective model of leadership may shift power to all levels and improve two-way communication. The previous Fire Service model (2010) talked about moving away from a traditional 'transactional' model of leadership towards a transformational approach as the best way to motivate staff to perform well, while the current leadership framework 'Inspiring: Leadership in the Fire and Rescue Services' clearly echoes the NHS approach (NFCC, 2017).

In practice, transformational leadership is not as common as the transactional style of leadership in emergency services organisations and they are not mutually exclusive. Several factors contribute to this situation emergency services are usually highly structured, have formalised and rigid promotion and recruitment systems with organisational cultures that emphasise compliance and conformity (Yates, 1999). Historically, emergency services have overwhelmingly promoted internally from within a hierarchical system and lateral entry to supervisory and senior leadership roles has been

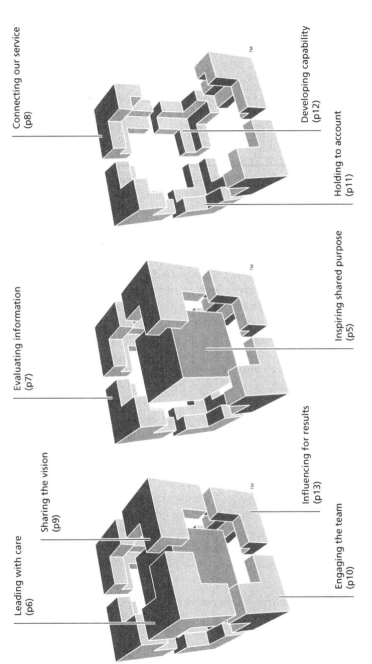

Figure 4.2 The nine dimensions of the Healthcare Leadership Model

Source: NHS Leadership Academy (2013: 4).

neglected for many years though it must be said that this has started to change gradually (Hill and Meyers, 2020).

The accompanying culture consequently is that of a strong compliance with organisational norms, rules, and hierarchy. Therefore, such dominant and collectively held beliefs often establish social identities with clear boundaries and stereotyping (see Owen, 2013; Kimmel, 2008; Owen et al., 2015; Lyng, 1995, 2000; Eyre, 2018; Granter et al., 2019). Efforts to bring about cultural change have proven to be difficult as longitudinal research has shown, especially in the ambulance services (see Wankhade, 2012; Wankhade and Brinkman, 2014; Wankhade et al., 2015; Wankhade et al., 2018; Granter et al., 2019). The two (culture and hierarchy) can combine to impose considerable inertia and resistance to change and can potentially isolate senior leadership from knowledgeable juniors (Yates, 1999). Managing within a chaotic, dynamic, and emotionally charged emergency environment can reinforce a traditionally 'reactive and commanding modus operandi of a unform culture' (Owen et al, 2015: 15). Such an 'heroic bias' in leadership research has also been attributed to be lack of empirical research linking leadership and risk (Fourie, 2022). Tourish (2013: 20–37) terms such bias as the 'excessive leader agency' which ascribes positive change to heroic leaders but hesitant to ascribe negative changes to at least partly good leaders (Fourie, 2022: 558). Mabey and Morrell (2011: 107) argue that 'heroic leadership theories tend to neglect context, reproduce normative control, overplay agency and fixate upon individual qualities, especially those which allow situations to be more effectively supervised and evaluated.'

In many quasi-military and rank-based organisations (including emergency services), the issue of 'power gradient' has been quite pervasive. It often acts as a hinderance to understanding the inter-relationships between human dynamics and can intensify the inter-personal risks faced by staff who want to question, speak up or share ideas or concerns with superiors (Flynn et al., 2008; Owen et al., 2015). Collinson (2012) discusses the notion of 'Prozac leadership' and 'power relationship between leaders and organisational members and the often ambiguous, asymmetrical, potentially contradictory and contested nature of such relations'. In his critique of power relationship between leaders and organisational members, Ladkin (2015) demonstrates how questions about power, authority and headship can be intricately related to the leadership and management styles and organisational structures

The organisational cultures within emergency services

A lack of nurturing and enabling organisational culture, coupled with high uncertainty avoidance and high power distance, is likely to result in a stifling climate which can be harmful to the organisation and can also heighten operational risks and blame culture (Owen et al., 2015; Wankhade et al., 2018; Wankhade and Brinkman, 2014). This is also true in the case of rank-based emergency services, which prioritise technical or operational skills over more softer skills, often ignoring issues around staff wellbeing and welfare at the cost of driving operational performance. Recent evidence has found increasing cases of stress, trauma, PTSD, sickness absence, and poor mental health in emergency services workers which have been further exacerbated by the current pandemic (Asghar et al., 2021; Wankhade and Patnaik, 2019; Heath et al., 2021; Greenberg et al., 2020 Wankhade et al., 2022).

The changing identities of professional culture(s) within the sector have prompted scholars to argue for a more compassionate and distributed leadership style(s) for managing a highly diverse, younger, impatient, and mobile workforce (see Wankhade and Patnaik, 2019; Wankhade et al., 2019). Recent explorations of more specific aspects of cultures across the ambulance, police, and fire services have highlighted more nuanced accounts from frontline staff and middle managers, which are at odds if not in conflict with those of senior leadership and are not always homogenous of what these organisations mean across the different occupational groups (see Charman, 2017; Wankhade et al., 2020; Brewis and Godfrey, 2019; Mansfield, 2015). However, more interestingly, these accounts are now challenging conventional wisdom on topics which till quite recently might have been considered as 'taboo', for instance, work intensity, job satisfaction, legitimacy, equality and diversity, racism, masculinity, public confidence, resilience. and wellbeing issues across organisations (see Loftus, 2022; McCann and Granter, 2019; Charman, 2019; Holdaway, 2019; Andrews and Ashworth, 2018).

Mees et al. (2016: 41) have argued that "in a world increasingly characterised by 'VUCA' factors (volatility, uncertainty, complexity and ambiguity), organisational leadership is typically seen as the key determinant of organisational culture." The notion of 'organisational climate', with its intellectual roots in the work of Koffa's behaviour environment (1935), has also been promoted as an important determinant of organisation's success (Altmann, 2000; Arabaci, 2010) and the shared elements of organisational culture and climate are broadly associated in recent literature on leadership practice (see Sani, 2012). Managing organisational climate has also helped to embed resilience practices in organisations (Mees et al., 2016).

Overcoming dysfunctional momentum

Turner (1976) in his classic study of the development of disasters, posits 'failures of foresight' as a cause of many accidents, a failure to notice critical cues that suggest change is needed (Salancik, 1977; Weick and Sutcliffe,

2007). A contrasting perspective is however provided by Barton and Sutcliffe (2009: 1330–1331), who argue that individuals fail to take corrective action, not because they miss cues, but 'because they are so embedded in the unfolding situation that they fail to stop and incorporate those cues into a new understanding of that situation'. They suggest momentum implying lack of interruption in the tasks at hand and when individuals or teams continue to engage in a failing action, leading to undesired or incomplete ends, their actions become dysfunctional (Owen et al., 2015: 17). Emergency services often perform under testing conditions while dealing with a major incident or crisis and can get caught up in the socio-cultural context of their job and their identity including its media projections to be expected to 'get the job done' and can get caught up in this momentum (Granter et al., 2019; Lyng, 1990). Individuals and teams are more likely to redirect ongoing activities if they get the opportunity to stop and make sense of the situation in real time. Two critical social processes are important to trigger such interruptions: the first is giving voice to the concerns and the second is seeking alternative perspectives. Once interrupted, the actors can make unfolding situations 'sensible' and in the course of such re-evaluation, they can stop or change their original actions (Barton and Sutcliffe, 2009: 1348).

To conclude, it would seem that emergency services potentially have some inherent structural leadership problems and challenges but what can be done? Leadership practices in emergency services should tackle the challenges of 'power gradients' and 'dysfunctional momentum' highlighted in this section to address entrenched parties and cultural issues. We suggest a more collaborative approach to leadership in the following section.

Shared leadership approaches and their consequences

Conceptualisations around distributed, shared, collective forms of leadership have been put forward by a variety of scholars (see Brookes and Grint, 2010; Bolden, 2011; Harris, 2013) but they all share an emergent, interactive, and contextualised form of leadership process. Development of a more rigorous and systematic study of collective forms of leadership to deal with crisis situations has also been advocated (Hannah et al., 2009; Bøggild and Laustsen, 2016; O'Reilly et al., 2015a; Sanufentes et al., 2021). They call for further research as to how these alternate forms are organised and in what manner or stage they might help to better cope with the crisis, including development of positive characteristics associated with shared leadership approaches such as fast reaction capability and flexible response (Hannah et al., 2009).

In their study of the 33 Chilean Miners rescued in 2010, Sanfuntes et al. (2021) demonstrated how shared leadership played a significant role on dealing with the catastrophic events of 89 days through 'harnessing individual' capacities effectively and flexibly and activation of resilience pathways. The study concluded that 'by sharing responsibility and authority within the group, the miners were able to make better decisions and improve their capacity for adaptation and innovation to withstand the hard conditions of confinement' (p. 268. See also Teo et al., 2017; Usdin, 2014; Williams et al., 2017). In a related article, Useem et al. (2011) also highlight several leadership lessons from the handling of the crisis. Analysing the role of the Mining Minister Golborne during the crisis, the study pointed to the unequivocal focus on the objective of resolving the crisis by the top political team; the creation of multiple alternate paths for resolution of crisis (e.g. the three rescue shaft options) and the timely disclosure of information good or bad.

In contrast poor leadership, leadership failures and an inability to be proactive were cited as the critical and missing elements of Katrina response by the U.S. House Select Committee, which investigated the poor response to Hurricane Katrina (US Government, 2006). The 9/11 Commission found that the most important failure was 'one of imagination' (Waugh and Streib, 2006). This is particularly relevant given that the response to any major or widespread disaster now routinely involves effective coordination and collaboration between government agencies, an army of volunteers, charities, private firms, and first responders. For instance, the response to the 2006 floods in Northern England involved more than 600 agencies and organisations (Pitts, 2008). Serious coordination problems between the Federal Emergency Management Agency (FEMA), the U.S. Department of Defence and state of Louisiana was further cited by the Home Select Committee in response to Katrina (US Government, 2006). Similarly intergovernmental and inter-organisational coordination problems have been also raised in several other inquiry reports investigating major disasters such as the Manchester arena attacks in 2017 (Kerslake Report, 2018) and in academic studies (Murphy et al., 2020; Wankhade and Patnaik, 2019; Inglesby et al., 2001).

A focus on collaboration and cooperation is also central in the emergency management training programmes across many domains. For instance, FEMA staff routinely participate in courses to develop collaborative skills (Waugh and Streib, 2006; Lucas, 2005). In the U.K., the collaborative framework of the Joint emergency Services Interoperability Programme (JESIP) is underpinned by five core principles, namely co-location, communication, joint understanding of risk, coordination, and shared situational awareness to facilitate a joined-up approach by first responders (JESIP, 2016). Such formal communication and collaboration are also facilitated by personal relationships and familiarity between actors and first responders rather than simply by institutional contact (Waugh and Streib, 2006).

The need to develop and implement a more collaborative and compassionate leadership process during conditions of adversity has been advocated by several commentators and scholars, especially during the current pandemic (Greenberg et al., 2020). They share the view that leadership is an emergent, interactive, and contextualised process, involving multiple actors, in a dynamic situation of re-adjustment and re-calibration. Tourish (2020) has argued that the current pandemic has illustrated the ineffectiveness and limitations of the heroic and populist forms of leadership, which has been exalted in the literature to cope with the 'radical uncertainty' caused by COVID-19 in terms of deaths and economic collapse (see also O'Reilly et al., 2015a, 2015b; James et al., 2011). We therefore need to explore how shared forms of leadership can help to build resilient organisations able to cope with adversity (Sanfuentes et al., 2021; Grint, 2020; Tomkins, 2020; Usdin, 2014). Leaders play a central role in the coordination of tactical and operational planning during the handling of any crisis and this serves as a catalyst for followers to act resiliently (James and Wooten, 2005). Shared or distributed forms of leadership can be critical to the 'achievement of effective performance in situations of crisis because the emergence of different leaders improves the collective's responsiveness to them since followers work at the front line, closer to external actors, they are able to make sense of and react to critical contingencies faster and more flexibly than formal leaders can' (Sanfuentes et al., 2021: 257; but see also Hannah et al., 2009; Klein et al., 2006).

Conclusion

Emergency services leadership operates in a dynamic and unstable terrain, often requiring quick decision making under pressure in a crisis. This places a lot of responsibility on leaders to make the correct call. Notwithstanding the current focus on a shared and distributed approach to leadership within the sector, the notions of 'rank and authority' still remain deep rooted and reflect command-and-control management styles and structures (Davis and Bailey, 2018; Herrington and Colvin, 2016; Loftus, 2010). It is not our intention to suggest or argue that charismatic or transformational leadership styles are no longer relevant or do not serve a purpose within extreme contexts. They do and the importance of more transformational or 'heroic' models of leadership while dealing with a crisis and in more wider settings has been well documented in leadership studies. On the contrary, our key argument in this chapter has been to an extent about a recalibration of leadership theory and practice within the extreme context. This echoes debates in the mainstream leadership discourse, about exploring how leadership is exercised and articulated in new organisational forms which are relational, community, and network based (see Santos and Eisenhardt, 2005; Nahapiet, 2008; Mabey and Morrell, 2011; Orlikowski, 2002). We also concur with Iszatt-White (2011)'s call for a more context-rich understanding of leadership in action.

In this chapter, we have promoted the merits of a more collaborative and shared approaches to leadership which we consider are better suited to the very challenging emergency services environment mitigated by a contested policy agenda, reducing organisational budgets and challenges in form of the pandemics and new disasters. In so doing, we have drawn attention to the increasingly complex nature of extreme events and taken into account the evidence supporting a collaborative approach to emergency management and learning from recent major disasters (such as 9/11 Commission, Hurricane Katrina Manchester Arena attack, and many more).

There is much to be applauded in the emergency services, and they have constantly developed and evolved to meet the demands they face. However, our analysis and current evidence clearly point out there are significant areas where further 'improvement in the leadership capability of emergency services would enhance the working of the staff and personnel in those services and also improve the ability of these services to meet the challenges of a fast-changing world' (Yates, 1999: 64; Wankhade et al., 2019; McCann and Granter, 2019). We agree with Hannah et al. (2009: 914) that the manner and effectiveness with which new leaderships operate will be contextualised and that the unique qualities and characteristics of extreme contexts will create contingencies that alter the relationships between constructs in these theories; requiring conceptual understanding and new methodologies to guide future theory-building and research. A call for more empirical research in extreme contexts including efforts to develop new theoretical models follow from this analysis.

References

Altmann, R. (2000). Understanding organizational climate: Start minimizing your workforce problems. *Water Engineering & Management*, 147(6): 31–32.

Andrews, R., and Ashworth, R. (2018). Feeling the heat? Management reform and workforce diversity in the English fire service. In P. Murphy and G. Greenhalgh (eds.), *Fire and Rescue Services: Leadership and Management Perspectives*, 145–158. Geneva, Switzerland: Springer.

Arabaci, I.B. (2010). Academic and administration personnel's perceptions of organizational climate. *Procedia—Social and Behavioral Sciences*, 2: 4445–4450.

Asghar, Z., Wankhade, P., Bell, F., Sanderson, K., Hird, K., Phung, V.-H., and Siriwardena, N. (2021). Trends, variations and prediction of staff sickness absence rates among NHS ambulance services in England: A time series study. *BMJ Open* (forthcoming). DOI: 10.1136/bmjopen-2021-053885

Avolio, B.J., Keng-Highberger, F.T., Lord, R.G., Hannah, S.T., Schaubroeck, J.M., and Kozlowski, S.W.J. (2022). How leader and follower prototypical and anti-typical attributes influence ratings of transformational leadership in an extreme context. *Human Relations*, 75(3): 441–474.

Barton, M.A., and Kahn, W. (2019). Group resilience: The place and meaning of relational pauses. *Organization Studies*, 40(9): 1409–1429.

Barton, M.A., and Sutcliffe, K.L. (2009). Overcoming dysfunctional momentum: Organizational safety as a social achievement. *Human Relations*, 62(9): 1327–1356.

Barton, M.A., Vogus, K.T., and DeWitt, T. (2015). Performing under uncertainty: Contextualized engagement in wildland firefighting. *Journal of Contingencies and Crisis Management*, 23(2): 74–83.

Bass, B.M. (1998). *Transformational Leadership: Industrial, Military, and Educational Impact*. Mahwah, NJ: Lawrence Erlbaum Associates.

Bass, B.M. (2008). *Bass' Handbook of Leadership: Theory, Research and Managerial Applications*. New York: Free Press.

Bøggild, T., and Laustsen, L. (2016). An intra-group perspective on leader preferences: Different risks of exploitation shape preferences for leader facial dominance. *The Leadership Quarterly*, 27: 820–837.

Bolden, R. (2011). Distributed leadership in organizations: A review of theory and research. *International Journal of Management Reviews*, 13(3): 251–269.

Bolden, R., Petrov, G., and Gosling, J. (2009). Distributed leadership in higher education: Rhetoric and reality. *Educational Management, Administration and Leadership*, 37(2): 257–277.

Brewis, J., and Godfrey, R. (2019). From extreme to mundane? The changing face of paramedicine in the UK ambulance service. In P. Wankhade, L. McCann, and P. Murphy (eds.), *Critical Perspectives on the Management and Organization of Emergency Services*, 179–199. Abingdon: Routledge.

Brookes, S., and Grint, K. (2010). *The New Public Leadership Challenge*. New York: Palgrave Macmillan.

Brunetto, Y., Farr-Wharton, B., Wankhade, P., Saccon, C., and Xerri, M. (2022). Managing emotional labour: The importance of organisational support for managing police officers in England and Italy. *The International Journal of Human Resource Management* (forthcoming). DOI: 10.1080/09585192.2022.2047755

Burke, C.S., Shuffler, M.L., and Wiese, C.W. (2018). Examining the behavioural and structural characteristics of team leadership in extreme environments. *Journal of Organizational Behaviour*, 36(6): 716–730.

Caro, D.H.J. (2016). Towards transformational emergency systems leadership: A holonic perspective. *International Journal of Healthcare*, 2(1): 1–5.

Charman, S. (2017). *Police Socialisation, Identity and Culture: Becoming Blue*. Basingstoke: Palgrave.

Charman, S. (2019). Changing landscapes, changing identities—Policing in England and Wales. In P. Wankhade, L. McCann, and P. Murphy (eds.), *Critical Perspectives on the Management and Organization of Emergency Services*. Abingdon: Routledge.

College of Policing (2015). *Leadership Review: Recommendations For delivering Leadership at All Levels*. Ryton-on-Dunmore: College of Policing.

College of Policing. (2017). *Guiding Principles for Organisational Leadership*. Ryton-on-Dunmore: College of Policing.

Collinson, D. (2012). Prozac leadership and the limits of positive thinking. *Leadership*, 8(2): 87–107.

Cooke, F.L., Cooper, B., Bartram, T., Wang, J., and Mei, H. (2019). Mapping the relationships between high-performance work systems, employee resilience and engagement: A study of the banking industry in China. *The International Journal of Human Resource Management*, 30(8): 1239–1222.

Crosby, B.C., and Bryson, J.M. (2005). A leadership framework for cross-sector collaboration. *Public Management Review*, 7(2): 177–201.

Crosby, B.C., and Bryson, J.M. (2010). Integrative leadership and the creation and maintenance of cross-sector collaborations. *The Leadership Quarterly*, 21(2): 211–230.

Crosby, B.C., and Bryson, J.M. (2018). Why leadership of public leadership research matters: And what to do about it. *Public Management Review*, 20(9): 1265–1286.

Davis, C., and Bailey, D. (2018). Police leadership: The challenges for developing contemporary practice. *International Journal of Emergency Services*, 7(1): 13–23.

Day, D.V. (2001). Leadership development: A review in context. *The Leadership Quarterly*, 11(4): 581–613.

Day, D.V., Fleenor, J.W., Atwater, L.E., Sturm, R.E., and McKee, R.A. (2014). Advances in leader and leadership development: A review of 25 years of research and theory. *The Leadership Quarterly*, 25: 63–82.

Day, D.V., Gronn, P., and Salas, E. (2006). Leadership in team-based organizations: on a threshold of a new era. *The leadership Quarterly*, 17: 211–216.

Dinh, J., Lord, R.G., Gardner, W.L., Meuser, J.D., Liden, R.C., and Hu, J. (2014). Leadership theory and research in the new millennium: Current theoretical trends and changing perspectives. *The Leadership Quarterly*, 25: 36–62.

Dionne, S.D., and Dionne, P.J. (2008). Levels-based leadership and hierarchical group decision optimization: A simulation. *The Leadership Quarterly*, 19(2): 25: 212–234.

Dionne, S.D., Gupta, A., Sotak, K.L., Kim, D.H., and Yammarino, F.J. (2014). A 25-year perspective on levels of analysis in leadership research. *Leadership Quarterly*, 25(1): 6–35.

Eyre, A. (2018). The making of a Hero: An exploration of heroism in disasters and implications for emergency services. In P. Murphy and G. Greenhalgh (eds.), *Fire and Rescue Services: Leadership and Management Perspectives*, 113–130. Geneva, Switzerland: Springer.

Farr-Wharton, B., Brunetto, Y., Wankhade, P., Saccon, C., and Xerri, M. (2021). Comparing the impact of authentic leadership on Italian and UK police officers' discretionary power, well-being and commitment. *Policing: An International Journal of Police Strategies and Management*, 44(5): 741–755.

Federal Emergency Management Agency (FEMA). (2004). *2004–2005 Training Catalog: Catalog of Courses for the National Fire Academy and the Emergency*

Management Institute Emmitsburg. Washington, DC: US Fire Administration/ FEMA.

Fisher, K., and Robbins, C.R. (2015). Embodied leadership: Moving From leader competencies to leaderful practices. *Leadership*, 11(3): 281–299.

Flynn, R., O'Connor, P., and Crichton, M. (2008). *Safety at the Sharp End: A Guide to Non-Technical Skills*. London: CRC Press.

Fourie, W. (2022). Leadership and risk: A review of the literature. *Leadership & Organization Development Journal*, 43(4): 550–562.

Granter, E., Wankhade, P., McCann, L., Hassard, J., and Hyde, P. (2019). Multiple dimensions of work intensity: Ambulance work as edgework. *Work Employment and Society*, 33(2): 280–297.

Greenberg, N., Docherty, M., Gnanapragasam, S., and Wessely, S. (2020). Managing mental health challenges faced by healthcare workers during COVID-19 pandemic. *British Medical Journal*, 368: 1211. http://doi.org/10.1136/bmj.m1211.

Grenfell Inquiry Report. (2019). *Grenfell Tower Inquiry: Phase 1 Report*. Available at: www.grenfelltowerinquiry.org.uk/phase-1-report

Grint, K. (2020). Leadership, management and command in the time of the Coronavirus. *Leadership*, 16(3): 314–319.

Gronn, P. (2002). Distributed leadership as a unit of analysis. *The Leadership Quarterly*, 13: 423–451.

Hannah, S., Uhl-Bien, M., Avolio, B., et al. (2009). A framework for examining leadership in extreme contexts. *The Leadership Quarterly*, 20(6): 897–919.

Harris, A. (2013). Distributed leadership: Friend or foe? *Educational Management Administration and Leadership*, 41(5): 545–554.

Heath, G., Wankhade, P., and Murphy, P. (2021). Exploring the wellbeing of ambulance staff using the 'public value' perspective: Opportunities and challenges for research. *Public Money & Management* (forthcoming). DOI: 10.1080/09540962.2021.1899613

Herrington, V., and Colvin, A. (2016). Police leadership for complex times. *Policing: A Journal of Policy and Practice*, 10(1): 7–16.

Hill, R., and Meyers, J. (2020). *Academic Literature Review of Direct Entry Into the UK Fire and Rescue Service (for NFCC)*. Birmingham: NFCC.

Holdaway, S. (2019). The professionalisation of the police in England and Wales: A critical appraisal. In P. Wankhade, L. McCann, and P. Murphy (eds.), *Critical Perspectives on the Management and Organization of Emergency Services*. Abingdon: Routledge.

Inglesby, T.V., Grossman, R., and O'Toole, T. (2001). A plague on your city: Observations from TOPOFF. *Clinical Infectious Diseases*, 32(2): 436–445.

Irons, B. (2017). Impact of a toxic leader on emergency services. *The Journal of Student Leadership*, 1(1): 11–15.

Iszatt-White, M. (2011). Methodological crises and contextual solutions: An ethnomethodologically-informed approach to understanding leadership. *Leadership*, 7(2): 121–137.

James, E., and Wooten, L. (2005). Leadership as (un)usual: How to display competence in times of crisis. *Organizational Dynamics*, 34(2): 141–152.

James, E., Wooten, L., and Dushek, K. (2011). Crisis management: Informing a new leadership research agenda. *Academy of Management Annals*, 5(1): 455–493.

JESIP. (2016). *Joint Doctrine—the Interoperability Framework (Edition 2—July 2016)*. London: Joint Emergency Services Interoperability Principles (JESIP).

Kerslake Report. (2018). *An Independent Review Into the Preparedness for, and Emergency Response to, the Manchester Arena Attack on 22nd May 2017*. Available at: https://www.kerslakearenareview.co.uk/media/1022/kerslake_arena_review_printed_final.pdf

Kimmel, M. (2008). *Guyland: The Perilous World Where Boys Become Men*. New York: Harper.

Klein, K., Ziegert, J., and Knight, A. (2006). Dynamic delegation: Shared, hierarchical, and deindividualized leadership in extreme action teams. *Administrative Science Quarterly*, 51: 590–621.

Knox, M. (2019). *Working in Dangerous Contexts: Conceptualising Leadership in Emergency Response Teams*. PhD thesis. Available at: https://nrl.northumbria.ac.uk/id/eprint/43801/ [Accessed 26 June 2022].

Koffa, K. (1935). *Principles of Gestalt Psychology*. New York: Harcourt Brace.

Kruke, B.I., and Olsen, O.E. (2012). Knowledge creation and reliable decision-making in complex emergencies. *Disasters*, 36(2): 212–232.

Ladkin, D. (2015). Leadership, management and headship: Power, emotions and authority in Organisations. In B. Carroll, J. Ford, and S. Taylor (eds.), *Leadership: Contemporary Critical Perspectives*, 3–25. London: Sage.

Loftus, B. (2010). Police occupational culture: Classic themes, altered times. *Policing and Society*, 20(1): 1–20.

Loftus, B. (2022). *Police Culture: Origins, Features and Reform*. Report prepared for the Mass Casualty Commission, March 2022. Available at: https://masscasualty-commission.ca/files/commissioned-reports/COMM0053825.pdf?t=1652281766

Lucas, V.J. (2005). *Analysis of Baseline Assessments: Emergency Management Accreditation Programme, 2003–2004*. Master's thesis, California State University, Long Beach.

Lyng, S. (1990). Edgework: A social psychological analysis of voluntary risk taking. *American Journal of Sociology*, 95(4): 851–886.

Lyng, S. (ed.). (2005). *Edgework: The Sociology of Risk-Taking*. London: Routledge.

Mabey, C., and Morrell, K. (2011). Leadership in crisis: 'Events, my dear boy, events'. *Leadership*, 7(2): 105–117.

Mansfield, C. (2015). *Fire Works: A Collaborative Way Forward for the Fire and Rescue Service*. London: New Local Government Network (NLGN).

McCann, L., and Granter, E. (2019). Beyond 'blue-collar professionalism': Continuity and change in the professionalization of uniformed emergency services work. *Journal of Professions and Organizations*, 6(3): 213–232.

Mees, B., McMurray, A.J., and Chhetri, P. (2016). Organisational resilience and emergency management. *Australian Journal of Emergency management*, 31(2): 38–43.

Murphy, P., and Dunn, P. (2012). *Senior Leadership in Times of Crisis. Noetic Notes*, vol. 3. ACT. Australia[RC224] : Noetic Group Pty Ltd.

Murphy, P., Wankhade, P., and Lakoma, K. (2020). The strategic and operational landscape of emergency services in the UK. *International Journal of Emergency Services*, 9(1): 69–88.

Nahapiet, J. (2008). There and back again? Organization studies 1965–2006. In S. Dopson, M. Earl, and P. Snow (eds.), *Mapping the Management Journey: Practice, Theory and Context*, 80–103. Oxford: Oxford University Press.

National Commission on Terrorist Attacks upon the United States. (2004). *The 9/11 Commission Report: Final Report of the National Commission on Terrorist Attacks Upon the United States*. New York: W.W. Norton.

National Fire Chiefs Council. (2017). NFCC *Leadership Framework: Inspiring Leadership in the Fire and Rescue Service*. Birmingham: NFCC.

NHS. (2013). *Healthcare Leadership Model: The Nine Dimensions of Leadership Behaviour*. Leeds: NHS Leadership Academy. Available at: https://www.leadershipacademy.nhs.uk/wp-content/uploads/2014/10/NHSLeadership-Leadership-Model-black-and-white.pdf

O'Reilly, D., LeitchHarrison, C.R., and Lamprou, E. (2015a). Introduction: Leadership in a crisis-constructing world. *Leadership*, 11(4): 387–395.

O'Reilly, D., LeitchHarrison, C.R., and Lamprou, E. (2015b). Leadership, authority and crisis: Reflections and future directions. *Leadership*, 11(4): 489–499.

Orlikowski, W. (2002). Knowing in practice: Enacting a collective capability in distributed organizing. *Organization Science*, 13: 249–273.

Owen, C. (2013). Gendered communication and public safety: Women, men and incident management. *Australian Journal of Emergency Management*, 28(2): 3–10.

Owen, C., Scott, C., Adams, R., and Parsons, D. (2015). Leadership in crisis: Developing beyond command and control. *Australian Journal of Emergency Management*, 30(3): 15–19.

Pitt, M. (2008). *Lessons Learned From the 2007 Floods*. London: Cabinet Office.

Porter, L.W., and McLaughlin, G.B. (2006). Leadership and the organizational context: Like the weather. *The Leadership Quarterly*, 17: 559–576.

Purba, A., and Demou, E. (2019). The relationship between organisational stressors and mental wellbeing within police officers: A systematic review. *BMC Public Health*, 19(1): 1286.

Salancik, G.R. (1977). Commitment and the control of organizational behavior and belief. In B.M. Staw and G.R. Salancik (eds.), *New Directions in Organizational Behavior*, 1–54. Chicago, IL: St Clair Press.

Sanfuentes, M., Valenzula, F., and Castillo, A. (2021). What lies beneath resilience: Analyzing the affective-relational basis of shared leadership in the Chilean miners' catastrophe. *Leadership*, 17(3): 255–277.

Sani, D.A. (2012). Strategic human resource management and organizational performance in the nigerian insurance industry: The impact of organizational climate. *Business Intelligence Journal*, 5(1): 8–20.

Santos, F., and Eisenhardt, K. (2005). Organizational boundaries and theories of organization. *Organization Science*, 16(5): 491–508.

Saunders, J. (2022). *Manchester Arena Inquiry*. Report of the Public Inquiry into the Attack on Manchester Arena on, 22nd May 2017, Vol. 2. London: Stationery Office. Available at: https://www.gov.uk/government/publications/manchester-arena-inquiry-volume-2-emergency-response

Schmutz, J., Lei, Z., Eppich, W., and Manser, T. (2018). Reflections in the heat of the moment: The role of in-action team reflexivity in healthcare emergency teams. *Journal of Organisational Behaviour*, 39(6): 749–765.

Sorokin, P.A. (1943). *Man and Society in Calamity.* New York: Dutton.

Stogdill, R.M. (1974). *Handbook of Leadership: A Survey of Theory and Research.* New York: Free Press.

Teo, W., Lee, M., and Lim, W. (2017). The relational activation of resilience model: How leadership activates resilience in an organizational crisis. *Journal of Contingencies and Crisis Management*, 25(3): 136–147.

Tomkins, L. (2020). Where is Boris Johnson? When and why it matters that leaders show up in a crisis. *Leadership*, 16(3): 331–342.

Tomkins, L., Hartley, J., and Bristow, A. (2020). Asymmetries of leadership: Agency, response and reason. *Leadership*, 16(1): 87–106.

Tourish, D. (2013). *The Dark Side of Transformational Leadership: A Critical Perspective.* London: Routledge.

Tourish, D. (2020). Why the coronavirus crisis is also a crisis of leadership. *Leadership*, 16(3): 261–272.

Turner, B.A. (1976). Organizational and interorganizational development of disasters. *Administrative Science Quarterly*, 21: 378–397.

Uitdewilligen, S., and Waller, M.J. (2018). Information sharing and decision-making in multidisciplinary crisis management teams. *Journal of Organizational Behaviour*, 36(6): 731–748.

Usdin, L. (2014). Building resiliency and supporting distributive leadership post-disaster: Lessons from New Orleans a decade after Hurricane Katrina. *International Journal of Leadership in Public Services*, 10(3): 157–171.

Useem, M., Jordan, R., and Koljatic, M. (2011). How to lead during a crisis: Lessons from the rescue of the Chilean miners. *MIT Sloan Management Review*, 53(1): 49.

US Government. (2006). *Hurricane katrina: A Nation Still Unprepared. Special Report of the Committee on Homeland Security and Governmental Affairs United States Senate.* 109th Congress. 2nd Session, SPECIAL REPORT S. Rept. 109–322. Available at: www.govinfo.gov/content/pkg/CRPT-109srpt322/pdf/CRPT-109srpt322.pdf

Wankhade, P. (2012). Different cultures of management and their relationships with organisational performance: Evidence from the UK ambulance service. *Public Money & Management*, 32(5): 381–388.

Wankhade, P. (2016). Staff perceptions and changing role of pre-hospital profession in the UK ambulance services: An exploratory study. *International Journal of Emergency Services*, 5(2): 126–144.

Wankhade, P. (2021). A 'journey of personal and professional emotions': Emergency ambulance professionals during COVID-19. *Public Money & Management* (forthcoming). DOI: 10.1080/09540962.2021.2003101

Wankhade, P., and Brinkman, J. (2014). The negative consequences of culture change management: Evidence from a UK NHS ambulance service. *International Journal of Public Sector Management*, 27(1): 2–25.

Wankhade, P., Heath, G., and Murphy, P. (2022). Re-imagining ambulance services through participation and deliberation. In J. Diamond and J. Liddle (eds.), *Reimagining Public Sector Management (Critical Perspectives on International Public Sector Management)*, 7: 139–155, Bingley: Emerald Publishing.

Wankhade, P., Heath, G., and Radcliffe, J. (2018). Cultural change and perpetuation in organisations: Evidence from an English emergency ambulance service. *Public Management Review*, 20(6): 923–948.

Wankhade, P., McCann, L., and Murphy, P. (eds.). (2019). *Critical Perspectives on the Management and Organization of Emergency Services*. New York: Routledge.

Wankhade, P., and Patnaik, S. (2019). *Collaboration and Governance in the Emergency Services: Issues, Opportunities and Challenges*. London: Palgrave Pivot.

Wankhade, P., Radcliffe, J., and Heath, G. (2015). Organisational and professional cultures: An ambulance perspective. In P. Wankhade and K. Mackway-Jones (eds.), *Ambulance Services: Leadership and Management Perspectives*, 65–80. New York: Springer.

Wankhade, P., Stokes, P., Tarba, S., and Rodgers, P. (2020). Work intensification and ambidexterity—the notions of extreme and 'everyday' experiences in emergency contexts: Surfacing dynamics in the ambulance service. *Public Management Review*, 22(1): 48–74.

Wansink, B., Payne, C.R., and Van Ittersum, K. (2008). Profiling the heroic leader: Empirical lessons from combat-decorated veterans of World War II. *The Leadership Quarterly*, 19: 547–555.

Waugh, W.L., and Streib, G. (2006). Collaboration and leadership for effective emergency management. *Public Administration Review*, 66(s1): 131–140.

Weick, K., and Sutcliffe, K.L. (2007). *Managing the Unexpected*, 2nd ed. San Francisco, CA: Jossey Bass.

Williams, T.A., Gruber, D.A., Sutcliffe, K.M., et al. (2017). Organizational response to adversity: Fusing crisis management and resilience research streams. *Academy of Management Annals*, 11(2): 733–769.

Yates, J. (1999). Leadership in emergency services. *Australian Journal of Emergency Management*, 129(1): 62–65.

5 The research-practice gaps in emergency services

Introduction and background

In 2012, the authors were part of the establishment of the *International Journal of Emergency Services* (IJES) and wrote and opening editorial entitled: 'Bridging the theory and practise gap in emergency services research: the case for a new journal' (Wankhade and Murphy, 2012). At that time police and criminal justice scholars were much better served in terms of the number of academic journals publishing their research than the two smaller 'blue-light' services (ambulance and fire and rescue services), although the interrelationships and interdependencies between the three main emergency services made their exclusion from the core purposes of the journal illogical. At the time there were a very small number of academic journals relating to emergency and disaster management, although this has since expanded, but there were relatively few journals that published articles on the management of the ambulance or fire and rescue services and even fewer that focused on these two services.

A decade ago, there was a demonstrable gap in the opportunities to publish research on the management of emergency services and one characteristic of the emergency service research that was published was its fragmented nature together with a clear theory-practice divide. The purpose of this chapter is to revisit the alleged gap between the discourse and interests of academic researchers and that of professional practitioners in the three emergency services and to assess the vitality and vibrancy of the research ecology and the strength of the inter-actions and inter-relationships.

In their study of the engagement of business practitioners with academic business research, Perea and Brady (2017) found a gap between academic research and businesspeople, but they also found that potential solutions to bridge the gap between academic journals and business practitioners should not be complicated to implement and would greatly help bring these two communities closer together, with mutually enriching results. One area

DOI: 10.4324/9781003198017-5

within business management that does have a significant literature on the research-practice gap is in the field of management accounting (e.g. Merchant, 2012; Laughlin, 2011; Kaplan, 2011; Scapens and Bromwich, 2010; Tucker and Leach, 2017; Tucker and Lowe, 2014; Tucker and Parker, 2014; Tucker and Schaltegger, 2016; Ferry et al., 2019). Adapting a conceptual model (Dudau et al., 2015) developed for investigating the research-practice gap in management accounting in public services (Ferry et al., 2019: 4), this chapter will analyse the state of the research-practice gap in the three blue light emergency services.

Before doing so, however, we need to acknowledge some significant contextual changes that have recently affected the emergency services, before describing the model and applying it to each of the three services. In simple terms, we will then compare the scholastic and professional landscapes and the changing nature and extent of the research-practice gaps in the three emergency services in recent years.

Contextual changes

Since the 2008/2009 recession, most advanced Western economies encouraged or guided by the World Bank, the International Monetary Fund, the European Commission, and the European Central Bank implemented economic policies colloquially known as 'austerity' policies which sought to reduce sovereign debt built up in response to the recession, via sustained and significant reductions in public investment and public spending (Blyth, 2013; Schui, 2014). In the U.K., the Coalition Government also sought to implement a parallel policy of empowering local authorities and public services to employ more discretion in how they delivered services. This parallel policy approach became known in the academic literature as 'austerity localism' (Lowndes and Pratchett, 2012) A number of countries, including the U.K., continued with these austerity policies for over a decade until the Coronavirus pandemic produced significant demands on healthcare and welfare systems and public expenditure almost inevitably increased. Despite the abnormal rise in expenditure due to the pandemic, the long-term funding of the emergency services and higher education institutions have effectively experienced significant long-term real reductions in central government financial support including support for research and innovation (NAO, 2015a, 2015b, 2017; Wankhade et al., 2019).

Over the same period devolution, decentralisation and subsequently 'Brexit' have significantly changed the organisational landscape and multi-level governance within the U.K., making them both more complex and more mutable (Murphy et al., 2020b). In addition, the increasing complexity in the nature of recent disasters, emergencies, and incidents has called for greater multi-agency cooperation or 'interoperability' between the three main emergency services and their collaborators with key partners as incidents become more complex and intractable, a trend illustrated by the Grenfell Tower Fire, the Manchester Arena Terrorist Attack, the Coronavirus pandemic, and the latest wildfire outbreaks due to extreme weather conditions (Murphy et al., 2020b; Wankhade and Patnaik, 2019).

In the higher education sector, another contextual factor is the traditional, long-term, and universal, adoption of the academic peer review process, that primarily relies on academic standards rather than the practical relevance of academic outputs (Nicolai et al., 2011). This is coupled with the international academic journal ranking systems that clearly value and promote theoretical over empirical work (Nkomo, 2009). These are powerful incentives for academics to undertake theoretical and conceptual research rather than empirical and practice relevant research. The demand for publication in three- and four-star journals has become almost ubiquitous in the annual assessment and promotion processes of universities and in their continual quest to ascend the increasingly international league tables for universities. So much so that in some countries, including the U.K., governments have recently required various national research assessments and applications for government-sponsored research grants to take into account and/or demonstrate the non-academic impact of their research outcomes (Parker et al., 2011; Research Excellence Framework, 2021a, 2021b).

The other contextual change relates to the extent and use of use of evidence in the public discourse, policy making and the public service delivery environments as well as in the quality assurance process and systems (McCann and Granter, 2019; Holdaway, 2019), the latter being necessary to reassure the public that public money is being appropriately spent by their representatives or agents in a democratic society. Whatever the historical balance between evidenced-based decision making or reliance on tradition, intuition, ideology, and/or ad hoc experience in political decision making there is little dispute that evidence-based policy making and practice in the U.K., the U.S., Europe, and elsewhere has been in retreat and has declined at all multi-government levels (Wells, 2018; French, 2018, 2019).

Both health and fire and rescue sectors have had long attachments and strong adherence to evidence-based policy and service delivery while the collection of evidence has always been central to the police and criminal justice system. In the U.K., policing saw a step change with the development on the 1970s of the Police National Computer which contains a database used by law enforcement organisations across the U.K. and now provides U.K. police forces with real-time online access to the database. In all three sectors another big driver of evidence-based decision making was the establishment of the Audit Commission in 1983 to transform the management of the public services, including the NHS (Campbell-Smith, 2008). The development of performance metrics, performance management and internal and external audit and inspection was increasingly evidence-based from the 1970s to approximately 2009/2010 when the use of evidence at national levels went into reverse and the use of tradition, intuition, ideology, and unsystematic experience re-emerged not just in England but across continents and under successive governments (Simons and Schniedermann, 2021).

Research—practice gap model

The public accounting field and the research-practice model developed by Dudua et al. (2015) share some characteristics with emergency services in that they are primarily interested in a public service, they have a clear evidence-based research tradition, they embrace applied research and have a strong tradition of practitioner engagement. The model identifies three groups or communities of interests. Although these groups are shown as separate groups on Figure 5.1 (our adaptation), in practice these are over-lapping groups of people, activities, and institutions. The first community of interest are research producers or providers consisting primarily of aca-demics or researchers in Higher Education Institutes (HEIs) or the research arms of various public organisations, public interest groups, or professional institutions. These are shown on the left in Figure 5.1.

On the right of Figure 5.1 are the research users or those that researchers seek to influence or address. These groups operate at multiple levels within most modern societies from the local to the regional and sub-national, to national and international levels. They include institutions, policy mak-ers, service deliverers, and practitioners as well as the third parties that are engaged in assuring the public about the activities of governments and pub-lic agencies that operate on behalf of the public and in the public interest. They include groups such as external auditors, inspectorates, and various scrutiny or standards agencies.

Both the research community and the practice community engage in either provider-initiated engagement or user-initiated engagement with the other community of interest and this is further facilitated, encouraged, or promoted through 'boundary spanning' institutions and associations and the types of bridging activity that is represented by the examples in the middle column. Again, the list of individuals and organisations on the diagram is illustrative rather than being in any sense comprehensive.

We have however adapted the model to include two of the contextual influences which we believe are acting as countervailing forces that may be operating against the closer realignment of research and practise. These are both taken from the contextual changes mentioned earlier and emblematic

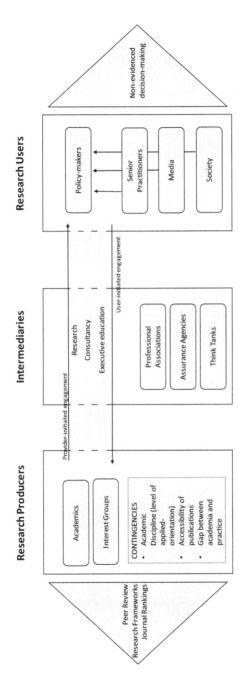

Figure 5.1 Research-practice gap model

Source: Adapted from Ferry et al. (2019). The Research-Practice Gap on Accounting in Public Services. Springer: Cham Switzerland, p. 4.

of those countervailing forces or changes in context. The first primarily relates to the research providers and producers and stems from the recent and increasing influence of international academic journal rankings, the academic peer review process, and the rise of research excellence assessments or academic performance regimes that all predominantly encourage and weight theoretical research more heavily than empirically based research. Although there has been some recent reaction to this influence, the overwhelming balance suggests that they are operating against the closure of the research-practice gap (Ferry et al., 2019).

The second is at the other end of our spectrum where there has been a recent but notable decline in the development and deployment of evidence-based policy and practice in the modern political and public discourses in North America, the U.K., Europe and other advanced western democracies. This has equally been evident in the blue light emergency services, local government and (to a much lesser extent) healthcare (Murphy et al., 2019, 2020a). In a very clear sense, we see this as operating against the closer realignment of research and practice.

Tucker (2019) in his contributions to the research-practice gap in accounting demonstrates the continuing asymmetry in the incentives for academics to undertake practice-related work and the difficulties of ensuring practitioner access to research findings through appropriate media or communication channels. Although he also acknowledges emerging changes to the more recent research assessments which increasingly seek to measure, monitor, and evaluate academic research impact, relevance, or societal usefulness, the predominant force or effect is away from closer realignment of research and practise (see also Parker et al., 2011).

Research-practice gap in the three emergency services

Ambulance services

Although paramedicine can be traced to the 1970s, the NHS in the U.K. only introduced a national course in 1986 and the national registration of professional paramedics in 2000. The establishment of the College of Paramedics followed in 2001. Although paramedics are not the only employees employed by the NHS and private ambulance services, they are at the core of the service's capacity for emergency response. This development period also coincided with the start of the change from the traditional view that ambulance services are intended to provide for the needs of the seriously sick or injured and primarily exist to efficiently transport patients to local hospitals (Department of Health, 2005; NAO, 2011, 2017; Pollock, 2013; Wankhade and Mackway-Jones, 2015). In the 21st century modern ambulance services need to demonstrate greatly enhance clinical capacities in order to absorb increased activity (including some previously undertaken by either primary and/or secondary care). This will also require reforms to operational and modern management as the role of the paramedic increasingly morphs into becoming a mobile healthcare provider (American Ambulance Association, 2008; Association of Ambulance Chief Executives, 2011). This need for transformation, articulated by Newton and Harris (2015), has generally been slow in its implementation in the U.K. (Wankhade et al., 2018, 2020) and has subsequently been highlighted by the services response to the Coronavirus pandemic (Wankhade, 2021).

In order to practise as a paramedic in the U.K. it now requires an approved degree in paramedic science or an apprenticeship degree and to be employed by an ambulance service as a qualified paramedic and be registered with the Health and Care Professions Council (HCPC). There are 35 universities in the U.K. offering paramedic science courses according to the Complete University Guide (2022) and this has recently increased although in 2022 the majority of courses, including the two top ranked courses, have had to use the national 'clearing system' to attract sufficient students to their courses starting in September 2022. There are now approximately 36,000 registered practitioners.

Despite this relatively large and growing potential community of interest, the number of paramedics and academics, engaged in management research and/or attending academic conferences, and the number of specialised events or specialised panels at wider national and international events remain small and have increased only marginally over the last two decades. Medical and clinical issues overwhelmingly dominate research outputs and there is very little management, interdisciplinary or international research on ambulance services in the non-medical literature. Historically there have been relatively few grants awarded to research the governance, leadership, management, or performance of ambulance services and relatively few academic journal articles, books or chapters published other than textbooks and manuals, although ambulance-related research is beginning to be published in top management journals (McCann et al., 2013; Granter et al., 2019; Wankhade et al., 2018, 2020; McCann and Granter, 2019).

This is also despite the prevailing clinical and medical culture (not least in the NHS) encouraging a very close research-practice nexus. There are also an encouraging number of potential boundary spanning institutions and/or types of bridging organisations and initiatives active or interested in the service. In addition to the HCPC and the College of Paramedics mentioned earlier, there are, for example, an Association of Ambulance Chief Executives and an Ambulance Service Group in the NHS Confederation. The Health Foundation is actively supporting and sponsoring new research focused on the ambulance trusts working with academic institutions. More broadly the service is inspected by the Care Quality Commission (as are non-emergency ambulance service) and falls under the remit of the National Institute for Health and Care Excellence which is a non-departmental public body originally formed in 1999, that publishes guidelines and standards and promotes good practice in all areas of Health and Social Care.

Why then has research not flourished and research practice nexus not disappeared or significantly reduced in this area? The service has strong public support and benefits from relatively benign or supportive media coverage in terms of both the news and service coverage in television programmes. During the current ongoing COVID-19 pandemic, ambulance response times have rocketed upwards causing unprecedented delays and there have been multiple reports of ever-larger queues of ambulances having to wait longer to transfer patients into already busy Accident and Emergency Departments, yet the news bulletins have largely remained sympathetic to the services.

Although the reasons for the continuing gap are undoubtedly numerous and complex, we suspect a large part of the answer lies in three areas or circumstances that are significantly influencing the development of ambulance services in the U.K.

The first is the relative size and weakness of the ambulance service and its delivery organisations (both within the NHS and contracting with the NHS) in relation to other service blocks and organisations within the NHS and Healthcare more generally. The relative size, influence and power of the primary care sector, or the hospital and secondary care sector and even the mental care and community care sectors, effectively dwarf the size and influence of the ambulance services with the NHS and healthcare. In addition to these asymmetrical power relationships the is the fact that the service has very little control over either the nature and pattern of patient and clients requiring the services assistance or the clinical settings to which they can be taken (NAO, 2017; Wankhade et al., 2020). The emergency ambulance service is almost wholly responding to demands outside of its control and has equally little control over the supply of potential healthcare settings to which it can take patients. This asymmetrical imbalance is then exacerbated by the relatively new, underdeveloped, and weak professional associations that represent the practitioners within the service, an issue explored in Chapter 2. The College of Paramedics, which is at the forefront of reform of practice, is still seeking 'chartered' status. These professional associations have been established but they currently cannot match the size, influence, or longevity of the equivalent professional associations elsewhere in the NHS or in healthcare generally.

The second issue is implied in the first issue when we refer to the established need but disappointedly slow transformation to a modern service.

This is partially a result of the continuing operational insularity associated with the service and the culture, outlook, and attitude of the service and its leadership and management (Wankhade, 2011; Wankhade and Mackway-Jones, 2015; Wankhade et al., 2018). Annual NHS staff surveys reveal serious and persisting concerns about ambulance staffs' physical and mental wellbeing. The service has rising absence, and vacancy rates, all consistently higher than in the other parts of the NHS (Asghar et al., 2021). As in other parts of the NHS there is a growing recruitment crisis, exacerbated by the U.K. leaving the EU and subsequent national policies on Immigration. All of these factors are leading to poor physical and mental health and low self-esteem and morale among paramedics (Heath et al., 2021) making service transformation that much more difficult.

The third factor, as we have argued elsewhere (Murphy et al., 2019, Wankhade et al., 2022), is the underdeveloped and relatively unsophisticated nature of the performance management regime for ambulance services and the associated internal and external inspection, scrutiny, reporting, and auditing arrangements (see also Wankhade, 2011). The performance management regime is a vital part of the infrastructure of the policy and delivery of public services. It should be an integral part of system, service and organisational improvement and development regime. It can also be a potential driver of service and/or organisational change if this is needed. A good system can enhance and encourage continual improvement and/or transformational change whereas a poor system can hamper or delay much-needed change. The underdeveloped and relatively unsophisticated nature of the regime for ambulance services exacerbates the limited power and discretion of the service and the slow transformation of the service helping to maintain the research-practice nexus for ambulance services.

Police services

In our second section given earlier, we noted that a significant change occurred in research in the management governance, leadership, and performance of police and policing with the development in the 1970s of the Police National Computer and the subsequent development of databases, performance metrics, and evidence-based research and practice from the 1970s. This improvement in data and information fuelled an expansion of academic interest in police and policing which also gradually reduced the research-practice gap in policing and criminal justice not least as the use of quantitative research methods increased. So much so that in our opening editorial to the *International Journal of Emergency Services*, referred to in this chapter's introduction, we noted that police and criminal justice scholars were much better served in terms of the number of academic journals available to publish their research.

Although evidence-based management research might generally have been in decline since our editorial appeared in 2012, the number of academics publishing management papers on police and criminal justice and the number of journals, conferences, events, and panels facilitating research in these areas has continued to grow, as has the number of undergraduate and postgraduate courses being offered. Of course, there are over a hundred law schools in the U.K. and many of them are well established but the number of police and criminal justice courses that are based in other disciplines and schools such as social sciences, social policy, politics, social work, psychology, and business and management schools has continued to increase.

The Complete University Guide for example now lists 37 universities in the U.K., where students can take undergraduate and postgraduate courses specifically in Forensic Science, all of which are very much practice based. As law has continued to attract students and researchers throughout this period, there is little doubt that research into policing has benefitted from the overlap with research on the wider criminal justice system. In parallel the Chartered Association of Business Schools Journal ranking lists which relate specifically to Business and Management Journals, and which are periodically revised (CABS, 2018), also shows a steady increase in journals that are primarily devoted to policing and the criminal justice system, and policing-related research has for some time featured in the top management journals. One of the contributory reasons for the latter is that interdisciplinary and international research has been developing and increasing as the nature of 'crime' changes.

If the research providers and research producers' community has continued to thrive, what is the situation in the 'bridging' community and what is happening in the practice community?

Crime and policing have attracted significant media coverage in terms of both factual and fictitiously based programming for many years. The recent rapid expansion and internationalisation of news, media outlets, television, and internet channels has generated an incredible demand for additional 'content' and ever greater interest in crime, detection, and policing. The Crime Writers' Association (CWA), a specialist authors' organisation in the U.K., was established in 1953 but now has over 900 members with a monthly magazine exclusively for members and a 'sister' organisation the Crime Readers Association.

If we take all forms of representations in all forms of the media, the service can be judged to have enjoyed a generally 'neutral' coverage. In more recent years public polls by members of the British Polling Council and Market Research Society have generally seen reduced public support for the police. This may partly because of increased political polarisation by the public and the fracturing of traditional political support patterns. There have always been multiple think tanks and interest groups as well as established professional and staff associations associated with the police and, unlike the ambulance service, these groups are long-standing sophisticated and powerful influencers.

Even 'new' bridging institutions and organisations such as the College of Policing (who took on training, and workforce related functions and the National Police Library) or the Independent Office for Police Conduct or Her Majesty's Inspectorate of Constabulary and Fire & Rescue Services (HMICFRS) are in fact successors to similar organisations that existed in the past seen by politicians as in need of reform. Thus, the College of Policing effectively was a replacement for the National Police Improvement Agency (NPIA), which itself replaced the Centrex (which included the National Centre for Policing Excellence and the Police Information Technology Organisation). The Independent Office for Police Conduct replaced the Independent Police Complaints Commission (IPPC), which itself replaced the previous Police Complaints Authority and HMICFRS replaced Her Majesty's Inspectorate of Constabulary (HMIC) which had been established since 1856 and some of the functions of the former Audit Commission.

Overall, the number and nature of the 'bridging' organisations have become more numerous and more defuse, and while they remain sophisticated and powerful influencers, the consensus among both academics and practitioners is that in the main the individual bridging organisations are not as powerful or as influential as some of their predecessors (Holdaway, 2019; Charman, 2019). This is partly because some of the previous organisations (NPIA, HMIC, IPPC, Audit Commission) were publicly funded as part of the service or sector infrastructure and assurance arrangements (previously referred to as the improvement infrastructure), while their replacements have been expected to operate on significantly reduced budgets with less access to political influence and weakened alignment to political parties. Self-funded or sector-funded agencies such as the Association of Police and Crime Commissioners or professional groups such as the Superintendents Association or the Police Federation are not as powerful or as well-resourced as in the past because membership numbers and hence subscriptions have dropped sharply, and the interest groups and think tanks are now operating in an increasingly crowded, fragmented, and competitive 'market'.

The impact of austerity and budgetary cuts has also had a profound effect on the police services and the constabularies (NAO, 2015a). Policing policy, service delivery, and assurance has become less integrated at national and local levels and there is increasing evidence of declining standards, most notably in the Metropolitan Police (Westmarland and Conway, 2020; Brown, 2021). As with the ambulance services over the last 10 years, the police service has seen rising absence, sickness, and vacancy rates and declining confidence and morale. Serious and organised crime, fraud, and corruption (particularly online and virtual crimes) and domestic and international terrorism are all increasing and increasingly complex to police. Civil disorder (which is heavily resource intensive) has risen and Brexit has meant the loss of international databases and information networks. Historical notions of police culture and identify have been questioned and re-interpreted (Lumsden, 2017; Cordner, 2017; Loftus, 2010; Charman, 2017).

A service that 10 years ago was developing a more open culture with increased collaboration, inter agency, and across agency performance improving (Murphy et al., 2019) is becoming more defensive and embattled with weakened assurance mechanisms and a detrimental effect on its service and organisational cultures. Unsurprisingly this has also led to a reduction in evidence collection and detection rates and evidence-based policy and delivery together with user-initiated engagement with the research providers and producers' community. Although academics appear keener than ever to engage with practice the research-practice nexus in police services is not closing as fast as it could and should do, and there are clear signs of it starting to reopen further.

Fire and rescue services

The fire and rescue services' communities of interest in the U.K. are roughly similar in size to the ambulance service in terms of both the practitioner and bridging communities of interest but is smaller in terms of the academic community. Although similar numbers are currently employed in ambulance and fire and rescue services, the numbers within ambulance services are increasing, as the demands on the services are increasing and sickness absence and vacancy rates are relatively high. The numbers employed in fire and rescue services have dropped by approximately 10% from around 56,000 in 2010 to 44,000 in 2022 (HMICFRS, 2021b). Nevertheless, the fire and rescue service remains one of the most popular services with the public and enjoys some of the highest trust and satisfaction ratings for public services anywhere in the world (HMICFRS, 2018). It also benefits from very positive and supportive media exposure both in terms of the news and in the services' depiction in factual and fictitiously based programming.

However, the academic community remains very small. The Complete University Guide does not list fire and rescue courses as a discipline and those that have full-time undergraduate courses are generally focused on fire engineering, materials resistance, trauma and health and safety rather than leadership and management. Post-graduate specialist courses such as Fire Scene Investigation or Trauma Informed Practice are generally within the same institutions or offered by institutions that have medical and clinical courses in the case of the latter. Most fire and rescue services therefore must look to public sector management courses or more generic leadership and management courses for their managerial development. Full- and part-time public management courses are declining in numbers, while the MBA and postgraduate management courses are increasing although the number of students from fire services at the latter is declining as learning and teaching budgets have been squeezed and basic training such as on Breathing Apparatus, Fire Safety and Building Regulation and Fire Engineering have to take priority.

In addition, multiple promises by the government since 2010 to improve the data and information available to the sector and its services at national and local levels have not materialised and the evidence base for new and applied research has therefore deteriorated (Murphy and Greenhalgh, 2018; Murphy et al., 2019, 2020a). This means that the small academic community has at best been static but has probably seen a small decline over the period since the *International Journal of Emergency Services* was established in 2012. The number of academics and practitioners engaged in management research and/or attending academic conferences and the number conferences and specialised events or specialised panels at wider national and international events is also static at best.

For many years all fire and rescue services also leaned heavily on the Fire Service College for their regular practical and technical training and for continual professional development. They also looked to the Emergency Planning College for their emergency planning and incident management courses (as did their colleagues from police, ambulance, and public health and local authorities). Both institutions have been operating at reduced capacity as a result of public sector budgetary reductions since 2010. Since 2010 the Emergency Planning College has been operated on behalf of the Cabinet Office by Serco, a public limited company that derives its main income from outsourced government contracts in health, transport, justice, immigration, and defence. The Fire Service College, which was opened by the Home Office in 1968, provided the full range of training for firefighters at all levels, from initial training for newly recruited firefighters through to training and development for senior leadership and management. In 2013, Fire Service College was sold to Capita, the largest business process outsourcing and professional services company in the U.K.

In their heydays both the Fire Service College and the Emergency Planning College were in effect two of the most important and active members of the sectors 'bridging' community with the former also having an international role as it provided leadership, command, and technical training to Fire and Civil Defence Authorities around the world. Its headquarter has lecture facilities and specialised areas such as I.T. suites, a chemistry laboratory, and hydraulics laboratory and a large fire ground where practical drills can be undertaken as it is sited on a 500-acre former airfield. It was a member of the European Fire Service Colleges' Association and hosted domestic and international conferences for both academics and practitioners.

The college is also the administrative base of another important bridging organisation, the Fire Protection Association (FPA), which is the U.K.'s national fire safety organisation and the Institute of Fire Engineers held its annual conference of Fire-Related Research and Development at the college for many years before moving to West Midlands Fire Service H.Q. in 2017.

In 2011, recognising the numerous but generally small and insular interest groups in the sector, the Fire Sector Federation was formed to 'to give voice to and exert influence in shaping future policy and strategy related to the UK Fire Sector'. The federation is a 'not for profit' non-government organisation which brings together representatives from the wide range of stakeholders which make up the U.K. fire sector. At the time it was established the (then) Coalition Government made it clear that it no longer intended to control and direct the way fire and rescue services are delivered and instead expected the fire sector to take a lead in shaping policy.

Since that time other organisations and institutes that also operate as boundary spanners have been established such as the National Fire Chiefs Council, the HMICFRS, and the Fire Standards Board but as with the police service these organisations are largely re-creations and/or successors to similar organisations that existed in the past but seen by politicians as in need of reform. Thus, HMICFRS mentioned earlier in relation to the police, not only replaced HMIC but also the former Fire Service Inspectorate role and some roles of the Audit Commission. The National Fire Chiefs Council replaced the Chief Fire Officers Association and took over some minor responsibilities and roles from the Home Office.

The fire sector was for many years known for its strong professional and representative bodies exemplified by the Fire Brigades Union and to an extent they played a boundary spanning role, although this role was very subservient to their main representative role. On occasion they also commissioned or collaborated in research with the academic community. Similarly, there was a small stream of direct commissions from local Fire and Rescue services (Mansfield, 2015). As in the police service successor organisations that are publicly funded have tended to be less powerful, less influential with smaller budgets than the former organisations they replaced while self-funded or sector-funded organisations are not as powerful or as well-resourced as in the past because membership numbers and hence sub-scriptions have reduced.

Overall, in the fire and rescue sector the number and nature of the 'bridg-ing' organisations have become more numerous but (with the honourable exception of the Fire Sector Federation) they are now generally smaller organisations. They have predominantly remained low key and have not developed into the powerful influencers, that bridging organisations in the policing sector have. Despite commissions and contributions to recent high-profile inquiries which have directly affected the sector such as the Gren-fell Tower Fire (Moore-Bick, 2019; Prosser and Taylor, 2020), the Hackitt Review of the building regulations and fire safety (Hackitt, 2018) and the Fire Safety Act 2021 (which amends the Fire Safety Order) they remain relatively low key and probably not as influential as the public might expect.

In summary, with the numbers of active and potentially active researchers being employed in directly related courses declining, the bridging commu-nity becoming weaker and the practitioner community becoming smaller and less well-resourced, it is difficult to see how the research-practice gap can avoid growing, at least in the immediate future. This is despite the fire and rescue service generally adopting or developing a more outward-look-ing and collaborative organisational culture as it has responded to the years of government austerity policies and the subsequent challenges of the pan-demic (HMICFRS, 2021a, 2021b, 2021c; Murphy and Lakoma, 2022). A brief summary of the some of the current features of the three services is provided in Table 5.1.

Conclusions

In summary, our brief overview of the three emergency services after apply-ing the model devised by Dudau et al. to the three communities of interest finds that the research-practice gap in ambulance services is generally being maintained in a period of change which potentially provides an opportunity to see the gap closing. In policing, academics appear keener than ever to engage with practice and the research-practice gap may be closing but it is not closing as fast as it could and should do, and there are worrying signs that it may be starting to reopen. In fire and rescue services, we found that the size and influence of all three communities, researchers, practitioners, and bridg-ing organisations are either static or becoming smaller and in these circum-stances, it is more rather than less likely that the gap will grow at least in the short term. There are however in all three services some encouraging signs.

To conclude on a more optimistic note, it is very noticeable from domes-tic and international conference registrations that in all three academic com-munities the average age of colleagues actively engaged in research has

Table 5.1 Summary of Research-Practice Gap

Ambulance services

Research	Bridging	Practice
• Numbers of research academics static	• Agencies and institutions becoming engaged.	• Organisational/cultural change constant
• Courses, conferences, and PhD registrations increasing	• NHS culture favours research-practice nexus	• Clear standards and evidence-based practice
• More and better management journals accepting papers.	• Strongly positive public and media support	• Performance regime being reformed
		• A proactive College of Paramedics

Police services

Research	Bridging	Practice
• The numbers of research academics is increasing	• Multiple long-standing agencies and institutions with reduced influence	• Changing objectives and priorities generating uncertainty
• Courses, conferences, and PhD registrations are increasing	• Culture becoming more isolated and defensive	• Government support and infrastructure is eroding
• More and better management journals are accepting papers.	• Neutral or ambiguous media and reduced public support.	• Declining performance, confidence, and morale

Fire and rescue services

Research	Bridging	Practice
• The already small number of research (and teaching) academics is contracting	• Data and information availability (the evidence base) is relatively poor and static	• Services contracting in terms of operational employees, budgets and influence
• Courses, conferences, and PhD registrations are declining	• Agencies and institutions are still few and uncoordinated	• Government support and infrastructure is eroding
• More management journals are accepting papers, but numbers are static.	• Strongly positive public and media support	• Ambiguous objectives and priorities
		• A more outward-looking and collaborative organisational culture

significantly fallen over the period studies as a generation of experienced researchers have reach retirement ages and newer younger researchers replace them. There is an encouraging move towards more international and inter-disciplinary research across all three services, and most importantly, in our view, the continuously changing nature of the incidents and challenges all three services face will itself generate a greater need, demand, and opportunity for research and the reduction of the research-practice gaps.

References

American Ambulance Association. (2008). *Structure for Quality: Best Practices in Designing, Managing and Contracting for Emergency Ambulance Service*. McLean: American Ambulance Association.

Asghar, Z., Wankhade, P., Bell, F., Sanderson, K., Hird, K., Phung, V.-H., and Siriwardena, N. (2021). Trends, variations and prediction of staff sickness absence rates among NHS ambulance services in England: A time series study. *BMJ Open*. https://bmjopen.bmj.com/content/11/9/e053885

Association of Ambulance Chief Executives. (2011). *Taking Healthcare to the Patient 2: A Review of Six Years' Progress and Recommendations for the Future*. London: Association of Ambulance Chief Executives.

Blyth, M. (2013). *Austerity: The History of a Dangerous Idea*. Oxford: Oxford University Press.

Brown, J. (2021). *Policing in the UK Research Report No. 8582 House of Commons Library*. London: TSO.

Campbell-Smith, D. (2008). *Follow the Money: The Audit Commission, Public Money and the Management of Public Services 1983–2008*. London: Allen Lane.

Charman, S. (2017). *Police Socialisation, Identity and Culture: Becoming Blue*. Basingstoke: Palgrave.

Charman, S. (2019). Changing landscapes, changing identities—Policing in England and Wales. In P. Wankhade, L. McCann, and P. Murphy (eds.), *Critical Perspectives on the Management and Organization of Emergency Services*. Abingdon: Routledge.

Chartered Association of Business Schools. (2018). *CABS Academic Journal Guide*. Available at: https://charteredabs.org/academic-journal-guide-2018/ [Accessed 2 August 2022].

Complete University Guide. (2022). *New 2023 League Tables: Independent UK University Rankings, Course Information and Expert Advice for Every Student*. Available at: www.thecompleteuniversityguide.co.uk/ [Accessed 2 August 2022].

Cordner, G. (2017). Police culture: Individual and organizational differences in police officer Perspectives. *Policing: An International Journal of Police Strategies & Management*, 40(1): 11–25.

Department of Health DH. (2005). *Taking Healthcare to the Patients: Transforming NHS Ambulance Services*. London: Department of Health.

Dudau, A., Korac, S., and Saliterer, I. (2015). *Mapping Current Engagement— Bridging the Academic-Practitioner Gap*. IRSPM SIG Accounting and Accountability. Nottingham Trent University.

Ferry, L., Saliterer, I., Steccolini, I., and Tucker, B. (2019). *The Research-Practice Gap on Accounting in Public Services*. Cham, Switzerland: Springer.

French, R. (2018). Lessons from the evidence on evidence-based policy. *Canadian Public Administration*, 61(3): 425–442.

French, R. (2019). Is it time to give up on evidence-based policy? Four answers. *Policy & Politics*, 47(1): 151–168.

Granter, E., Wankhade, P., McCann, L., Hassard, J., and Hyde, P. (2019). Multiple dimensions of work intensity: Ambulance work as edgework. *Work Employment and Society*, 33(2): 280–297.

Hackitt, J. (2018). *Building a Safer Future Independent Review of Building Regulations and Fire Safety: Final Report, Cmnd 9607*. London: TSO.

Heath, G., Wankhade, P., and Murphy, P. (2021). Exploring the wellbeing of ambulance staff using the 'public value' perspective: Opportunities and challenges for research. *Public Money & Management*. http://doi.org/10.1080/09540962.2021.1899613.

HMICFRS. (2018). *Public Perceptions of Fire and Rescue Services in England 2018*. London: HMICFRS.

HMICFRS. (2021a). *COVID-19 Inspection Letters*. Available at: https://www.justiceinspectorates.gov.uk/hmicfrs/search?sector=fire&cat=&frs=&year=&month=&s=%20Covid&type=publications [Accessed 18 November 2022].

HMICFRS. (2021b). *Responding to the Pandemic: The Fire and Rescue Service's Response to the COVID-19 Pandemic in 2020*. London: HMICFRS.

HMICFRS. (2021c). *State of Fire and Rescue—the Annual Assessment of Fire and Rescue Services in England 2020, HMICFRS*. London: HMICFRS.

Holdaway, S. (2019). The professionalisation of the police in England and Wales: A critical appraisal. In P. Wankhade, L. McCann, and P. Murphy (eds.), *Critical Perspectives on the Management and Organization of Emergency Services*. Abingdon: Routledge.

Kaplan, R.S. (2011). Accounting knowledge that advances professional knowledge and practice. *The Accounting Review*, 86(2): 367–383.

Laughlin, R.C. (2011). Accounting research policy and practice: Worlds together or worlds apart? In E. Evans, R. Burritt, and J. Guthrie (eds.), *Bridging the Gap Between Academic Accounting Research and Professional Practice*, 23–30. Sydney: Centre for Governance and Sustainability, University of Sydney Australia and the Institute of Chartered Accountants of Australia.

Loftus, B. (2010). Police occupational culture: Classic themes, altered times. *Policing and Society*, 20(1): 1–20.

Lowndes, V., and Pratchett, L. (2012). Local government under the coalition government: Austerity, localism and the big society. *Local Government Studies*, 38(1): 21–40.

Lumsden, K. (2017). It's a profession, it isn't a job': Police officers' views on the professionalisation of policing in England. *Sociological Research Online*, 22(3): 4–20.

Mansfield, C. (2015). *Fire Works: A Collaborative Way Forward for the Fire and Rescue Service*. London: New Local Government Network (NLGN).

McCann, L., and Granter, E. (2019). Beyond 'blue-collar professionalism': Continuity and change in the professionalization of uniformed emergency services work. *Journal of Professions and Organizations*, 6(3): 213–232.

McCann, L., Granter, E., Hyde, P., and Hassard, J. (2013). Still blue-collar after all these years? An ethnography of the professionalization of emergency ambulance work. *Journal of Management Studies*, 50: 750–776.

Merchant, K.A. (2012). Making management accounting research more useful. *Pacific Accounting Review*, 24(3): 1–34.

Moore-Bick, M. (2019). *Grenfell Tower Inquiry: Phase 1 Report*. London: TSO.

Murphy, P., Ferry, L., Glennon, R., and Greenhalgh, K. (2019). *Public Service Accountability: Rekindling a Debate*. Cham, Switzerland: Palgrave Macmillan.

Murphy, P., and Greenhalgh, K. (eds.). (2018). *Fire and Rescue Services: Leadership and Management Perspectives*. New York: Springer.

Murphy, P., and Lakoma, K. (2022). How did fire and rescue services in England respond to the COVID-19 pandemic? *International Journal of Emergency Services*. http://doi.org/10.1108/IJES-10-2021-0070

Murphy, P., Lakoma, K., Eckersley, P., and Glennon, R. (2020a). A sinking platform: The data dilemma. Chapter 3 in *Rebuilding the Fire and Rescue Services: Policy, Delivery and Assurance*. Emerald points. Bingley: Emerald Publishing Limited.

Murphy, P., Wankhade, P., and Lakoma, K. (2020b). The strategic and operational landscape of emergency services in the UK. *International Journal of Emergency Services*, 9(1): 69–88.

National Audit Office NAO. (2011). *Transforming NHS Ambulance Services*. London: TSO.

National Audit Office. (2015a). *Financial Sustainability of Police Forces in England and Wales*. Available at: www.nao.org.uk/wp-content/uploads/2015/06/Financial-sustainability-of-policeforces.pdf

National Audit Office. (2015b). *Impact of Funding Reductions on Fire and Rescue Services*. Available at: www.nao.org.uk/report/impact-of-funding-reductions-onfire-and-rescue-services/

National Audit Office. (2017). *NHS Ambulance Services*. London: National Audit Office.

Newton, A., and Harris, G. (2015). Leadership and system thinking in the modern ambulance service. Chapter 7 in P. Wankhade and K. Mackway-Jones (eds.), *Ambulance Services: Leadership and Management Perspectives*. Cham, Switzerland: Springer.

Nicolai, A.T., Schulz, A.C., and Gobel, M. (2011). Between sweet harmony and a clash of cultures: Does a joint academic-practitioner review reconcile rigour and relevance? *Journal of Applied Behavioral Science*, 47(1): 53–75.

Nkomo, S. (2009). The seductive power of academic journal rankings: Challenges of searching for the otherwise. *Academy of Management Learning & Education*, 8(1): 106–112.

Parker, L.D., Guthrie, J., and Linacre, S. (2011). Editorial: The relationship between academic accounting research and professional practice. *Accounting, Auditing & Accountability Journal*, 24(1): 5–14.

Perea, E., and Brady, M. (2017). Research rigor and the gap between academic journals and business practitioners. *Journal of Management Development*, 36(8): 1052–1062.

Pollock, A.C. (2013). Ambulance services in London and Great Britain from 1860 until today: A glimpse of history gleaned mainly from the pages of contemporary journals. *Emergency Medicine Journal*, 30(2): 218–222.

Prosser, T., and Taylor, M. (2020). *The Grenfell Tower Fire: Benign Neglect and the Road to an Avoidable Tragedy.* Shoreham by Sea: Pavilion Publishing.

Research Excellence Framework. (2021a). *Panel Criteria and Working Methods REF 2019/02.* Available at: www.ref.ac.uk [Accessed 29 July 2022].

Research Excellence Framework. (2021b). *Guidance on Submissions Part 3 Section 3 REF 2019/01.* Available at: www.ref.ac.uk [Accessed 29 July 2022].

Scapens, R.W., and Bromwich, M. (2010). Editorial. Practice, theory and paradigms. *Management Accounting Research*, 21(2): 77–78.

Schui, F. (2014). *Austerity: The Great Failure.* New Haven: Yale University Press.

Simons, A., and Schniedermann, A. (2021). The neglected politics behind evidence-based policy: Shedding light on instrument constituency dynamics. *Policy and Politics*, 49(4): 513–529.

Tucker, B.P. (2019). Where there's a will. . . . the research-practice gap in accounting. Chapter 2 in L. Ferry, I. Saliterer, I. Steccolini, and B. Tucker (eds.), *The Research Practice Gap on Accounting in Public Services.* Cham, Switzerland: Springer.

Tucker, B.P., and Leach, M. (2017). Learning from the experience of others: Lessons from the research-practice gap in management accounting. *Advances in Management Accounting*, 29: 127–181.

Tucker, B.P., and Lowe, A.D. (2014). Practitioners are from Mars; academics are from Venus? An empirical investigation of the research-practice gap in management accounting. *Accounting, Auditing & Accountability Journal*, 29(3): 362–400.

Tucker, B.P., and Parker, L.D. (2014). In our ivory tower? The research-practice gap in management accounting: An academic perspective. *Accounting and Business Research*, 44(2): 104–143.

Tucker, B.P., and Schaltegger, S. (2016). Comparing the research-practice gap in management accounting. A view from the professional accounting bodies in Germany and Australia. *Accounting, Auditing & Accountability Journal*, 29(3): 362–400.

Wankhade, P. (2011). Performance measurement and the UK emergency ambulance service: Unintended consequences of the ambulance response time targets. *International Journal of Public Sector Management*, 24(5): 382–402.

Wankhade, P. (2021). A 'journey of personal and professional emotions': Emergency ambulance professionals during COVID-19. *Public Money & Management.* https://doi.org/10.1080/09540962.2021.2003101

Wankhade, P., Heath, G., and Murphy, P. (2022). Reimagining ambulance services through participation and deliberation. Chapter 10 in J. Diamond and J. Liddle (eds.), *Reimagining Public Sector Management: Critical Perspectives on International Public Sector Management.* Vol. 7, 139–155.

Wankhade, P., Heath, G., and Radcliffe, J. (2018). Cultural change and perpetuation in organisations: Evidence from an English emergency ambulance service. *Public Management Review*, 20(6): 923–948.

Wankhade, P., and Mackway-Jones, K. (eds.). (2015). *Ambulance Services: Leadership and Management Perspectives*. New York: Springer.

Wankhade, P., McCann, L., and Murphy, P. (eds.). (2019). *Critical Perspectives on the Management and Organization of Emergency Services*. New York: Routledge.

Wankhade, P., and Murphy, P. (2012). Bridging the theory and practise gap in emergency services research: The case for a new journal. *International Journal of Emergency Services*, 1(1): 4–9.

Wankhade, P., and Patnaik, S. (2019). *Collaboration and Governance in the Emergency Services: Issues, Opportunities and Challenges*. Cham Switzerland: Palgrave Macmillan.

Wankhade, P., Stokes, P., Tarba, S., and Rodgers, P. (2020). Work intensification and ambidexterity—the notions of extreme and 'everyday' experiences in emergency contexts: Surfacing dynamics in the ambulance service. *Public Management Review*, 22(1): 48–74.

Wells, P. (2018). Evidence based policy making in an age of austerity. *People, Place and Policy*, 11(3): 175–183.

Westmarland, L., and Conway, S. (2020). Police ethics and integrity: Keeping the 'blue code' of silence. *International Journal of Police Science & Management*, 22(4): 378–392.

6 Conclusion

Collaboration, not isolation, is the way forward

Scope and background

As we have highlighted in this book, emergency services provision is global in nature but the organisational and management research about their working, structures, people, etc., is still embryonic, evolving and frankly struggling to keep pace with the challenges that services are facing (Wankhade et al., 2019; Wankhade and Patnaik, 2019). The current body of empirical evidence remains relatively sparse and is still characterised by a clear theory and practice divide, something we argued over a decade ago (see Wankhade and Murphy, 2012). The first four chapters in this volume have documented the changing policy and organisational landscape and differences in the organisation and working of the emergency services; the state, pace, and style of recent attempts at professionalisation across the services; and interoperability and collaboration challenges for multi-agency cooperation. The discussion in Chapter 5 has highlighted some of the more positive management and governance attempts to improve services and drive efficiencies reflecting how these organisations have been buffeted by and are responding to the wider societal changes. Unfortunately, it has also highlighted severe resource challenges impacting on service delivery and the workforce.

In Chapter 1, we began by providing the recent context to the changing emergency services architecture, covering key policy changes and the changing socio-economic and political environment under which these organisations have to operate on a 24/7 basis. All three of the 'blue light' emergency services have changed significantly since the turn of the century, reflecting both the increased range and the changing nature of the risks that contemporary society and local communities now face. This has led to changes to the organisations themselves and how they are governed and managed. However, efforts to modernise these organisations have been accompanied by the emergence of a theory-practice research divide, resulting in a clear gap in the management understanding of these important public services,

DOI: 10.4324/9781003198017-6

which has itself further highlighted gaps in management and organisational research about each of these organisations. Emergency services have been particularly resistant to NPM in both theory and practice leading to the emergence of Public (and Social) Value within New Public Governance and New Public Service theories which reinstate public interest, public values, and the creation of public value as the focus of research and discourse.

Chapter 2 critically analysed the growing research interest in the sociological understanding of the origins and development of 'professions' in the organisations and 'professional' activities within the context of emergency services and the state of 'blue-collar' professionalism. The second half of the 20th century saw the rapid development of 'political science' as managerialism and institutionalism developed and managerialism in particular emphasised the value of *professional managers* and the concepts and methods they use. New public management meant that government was increasingly confined to facilitating, leading, and catalysing changes to achieve greater outputs with limited financial resources and fewer personnel. Efficiency rather than effectiveness, short-term and individual rather than long-term or collective goals, with little attention to inherent values or the public interest and the relegation of social and environmental concerns to economic performance (O'Flynn, 2007; Pollitt and Bouckaert, 2017; Lindgreen et al., 2019). With NPM persisting as the dominant theoretical influence over national and local government policy-making the critical exploration of the 21st century pursuit of professionalisation revealed a very mixed picture with different research practice gaps emerging in each of the three services. We concluded that notwithstanding the great strides made by emergency services to expand the scope of their practice and the increasing use of management techniques to drive efficiency and boost productivity, the claim for being considered as a 'profession' is still not fully realised in any of the three services and faces considerable challenges in both the police and fire and rescue services.

In Chapter 3, we examined the important but contested nature of emergency services collaboration highlighting conceptual difficulties such as problems of definition and scope and a variable understanding of the components of effective collaboration including the problems of measurement. We argue that fragmented governance and collaborative frameworks also remain a key stumbling block to a systematic understanding of the functioning of such collaborations. The current fiscal climate and the continuing demand for maximising efficiencies and reducing cost, is generating repeated calls for a more collaborative approach to emergency management beyond responding to major incidents and emergencies. Collaboration is increasingly acknowledged as a fundamental and inherent aspect of the emergency services operations (Wankhade and Patnaik, 2019;

Murphy et al., 2019) although some major inquiry reports have questioned the level of coordination and cooperation between the services, (US Government, 2006; Kerslake, 2018; Moore-Bick, 2019; Prosser and Taylor, 2020; Zaré and Afrouz, 2012). Drawing on the evidence of major inquiries such as the 9/11 Commission, Hurricane Katrina, and the Manchester arena bombing, we highlight measurement challenges and conceptual ambiguity amongst scholars as contributing factors or barriers to effective collaboration. We make the case for a clear rationale and objective evaluation of each collaboration coupled with rigorous assessment of the challenges and engagement by stakeholders. This leads us to advocate for agile and flexible leadership, effective stakeholder management and clearly defined scope and rationale to facilitate successful collaborations between emergency services.

The issue of emergency services leadership and culture is addressed in Chapter 4. The prevalence of a command-and-control style of governance, often accompanied by 'heroic' models of leadership in the sector, is partly due to the re-enforcement of such heroic characteristics by the popular press and media but also due to the paucity of empirical research and lack of theory building. The relative lack of systemic leadership research in 'extreme contexts' including the paucity of conceptual models was also highlighted along with the need for further research to develop new theoretical models. Nevertheless, our analysis suggests that there are significant areas where further 'improvement in the leadership capability of emergency services would enhance the working of the staff and personnel in those services and also improve the ability of these services to meet the challenges of a fast-changing world' (Yates, 1999: 64; Wankhade et al., 2018, 2019, 2020; McCann and Granter, 2019; Wankhade, 2021). We concluded that shared and distributed forms of leadership, taking into account the changing organisational, policy, and workforce dynamics, are likely to yield better results and we argue for a more meaningful and context-specific understanding to help theory building and model testing opportunities in identifying appropriate leadership styles. Further empirical research into extreme contexts to explore theoretical models in relation to the mainstream leadership and culture literature follows from this analysis.

In Chapter 5, we explored the research-practice gaps in the three emergency services in England and looked specifically at the last 20 years to revisit the alleged gap between the discourse and interests of academic researchers and that of professional practitioners. We adopted and adapted a relatively simple conceptual framework from the field of public service management accounting (which has a significant literature on the research-practice gap) and adapted it to look at the nature and scale of the gap in each of the three services and the potential for these to close in the future. The intention was to provide a roadmap or at least some ideas for a 'bridging' the theory-practice divide and this included identifying the 'bridging' role which can be played by a series of actors, agencies, or institutions such as community and volunteer organisations, think tanks, professional, and staff associations and government bodies and hence to embark on a collaborative research agenda to address such imbalance and raise the profile of emergency management research. We found the ambulance service going through a challenging period of change which at the least has the potential and provides the opportunity for closing the gap. In fire and rescue, we found that the gap is likely to widen at least in the short term, while in policing which potentially has the largest communities of interest in research, practice and in its 'bridging' community we found it is not closing as fast as it could and should do. This therefore remains a significant challenge as academia needs to be relevant to practice and practitioners need the legitimation of being theoretically robust (Ferry et al., 2019).

Conclusion and future research implications

We have previously suggested that while emergency service organisations are unlikely to enjoy the status, profile, and power of financial or consulting corporations, their influence is increasingly becoming wider and more prominent (McCann et al., 2019; see also McCann and Granter, 2019). Emergency services are becoming more commercialised through the adoption of sub-contracting, use of NPM-styled reforms, appointing business managers and management consultants, and the creation of volunteer roles (Granter et al., 2015). They are operating in an increasingly volatile risk environment, where social anxieties coupled with financial and operational pressures faced by emergency service workers are likely to persist, at least in the short term and immediate term. The public's general perception of the value of the blue light work continues to be positive albeit, at times, based on the discourse of the 'romantic', 'heroic', and 'masculine' nature of emergency service work (see also McCann, 2022; McCann et al., 2019).

While we have attempted to chart the professionalisation attempts by the emergency service organisations in Chapter 3 and provided some ideas for future of emergency services research in Chapter 5, the quintessential issue of the precise meaning and definition of an emergency worker still eludes us. Using a hermeneutic approach to the literature, Furness et al. (2020) provide six archetypes of the work of emergency paramedics namely paramedic as a 'stretcher bearer', as a 'hero', as 'male' as 'stoic', as a 'healer', as 'clinician' and as a 'storyteller'. A lot of this is reflected in the work of police officers and firefighters who often work in high-pressure working conditions in an emotionally charged environment requiring quick decisions, often in the media spotlight. Further research is, however, needed to explore the changing training needs of first responders in relation to responding to major incidents and for supporting their wellbeing and personal resilience (Wankhade, 2021; Santarone et al., 2020; Henderson and Borry, 2020; Wild et al., 2020). Notwithstanding the interoperability challenges we identify in Chapter 4, calls for further organisational research to explore how first responders might work together more effectively and better support the mutual wellbeing needs have gathered pace and need to be supported (James et al., 2022; Nelson et al., 2020).

As we argued at the outset, the aim of this volume was twofold: to advance the 'theory' of emergency management and analyse the implications for professionals and practitioners. Given the potential scope of the book, we have just managed to raise some of the key themes which address these twin objectives, and, like many other research projects, we are conscious that more could have been done, in terms of both scope and coverage. We sincerely hope that this volume will be useful to both the academic and the practitioner audiences. We made a conscious decision not to include issues of workforce health and wellbeing since these have been widely reported elsewhere and we wanted to avoid repetition (see Wankhade and Patnaik, 2019; Greenberg et al., 2020; Lawn et al., 2020; Heath et al., 2021; Wankhade, 2021; McCann, 2022).

Emergency services research is ripe for greater collaboration between academics, professionals, and practitioners to understand the role and contribution of these organisations which goes beyond simply protecting and saving lives. Our conceptual framework provides a way forward to bridge the clear 'theory-practice' divide. Further research can both test our hypothesis and also build upon our basic assumptions to enhance the state of research in emergency services management. It will also help us to understand the precise meaning, definition, and contribution of the emergency workers within their changing organisational, policy, and societal landscapes and acknowledges them as street level bureaucrats (Lipsky, 2010).

References

Ferry, L., Saliterer, I., Steccolini, I., and Tucker, B. (2019). *The Research-Practice-Gap on Accounting in Public Services*. Cham, Switzerland: Springer.

Furness, S., Hanson, L., and Spier, J. (2020). Archetypal meanings of being a paramedic: A hermeneutic review. *Australasian Emergency Care*. https://doi.org/10.1016/.auec.2020.08. 002

Granter, E., McCann, L., and Boyle, M. (2015). Extreme work/normal work: Intensification, storytelling, and hypermediation in the (re)construction of the New Normal. *Organization*, 22: 443–456.

Greenberg, N., Docherty, M., Gnanapragasam, S., and Wessely, S. (2020). Managing mental health challenges faced by healthcare workers during COVID-19 pandemic. *British Medical Journal*. http://doi.org/10.1136/bmj.m1211

Heath, G., Wankhade, P., and Murphy, P. (2021). Exploring the wellbeing of ambulance staff using the 'public value' perspective: Opportunities and challenges for research. *Public Money and Management*. https://doi.org/10.1080/09540962.2021.1899613

Henderson, A.C., and Borry, E.L. (2020). The emotional burdens of public service: Rules, trust, and emotional labour in emergency medical services. *Public Money & Management*. https://doi.org/10.1080/09540962.2020.183

James, L., James, S., and Hesketh, I. (2022). Evaluating the effectiveness of the fatigue and shift working risk management strategy for UK home office police forces: A pilot study. *International Journal of Emergency Services*. https://doi.org/10.1108/IJES-05-2021-0031

Kerslake, R. (2018). *An Independent Review Into the Preparedness for, and Emergency Response to, the Manchester Arena Attack on 22nd May 2017*. Available at: https://www.kerslakearenareview.co.uk/media/1022/kerslake_arena_review_printed_final.pdf

Lawn, S., Roberts, L., Willis, E., Couzner, L., Mohammadi, L., and Goble, E. (2020). The effects of emergency medical service work on the psychological, physical, and social wellbeing of ambulance personnel: A systematic review of qualitative research. *BMC Psychiatry*, 20(1): 348.

Lindgreen, A., Koenig-Lewis, N., Kitchener, M., Brewer, J., Moore, M., and Meynhardt, T. (2019). *Public Value: Deepening, Enriching, and Broadening the Theory and Practice*. Abingdon: Routledge.

Lipsky, M. (2010). *Street-Level Bureaucracy: Dilemmas of the Individual in Public Services*. New York: Russell Sage.

McCann, L. (2022). *The Paramedic at Work: A Sociology of a New Profession*. Oxford: Oxford University Press.

McCann, L., and Granter, E. (2019). Beyond 'blue-collar professionalism': Continuity and change in the professionalization of uniformed emergency service work. *Journal of Professions and Organization*, 6(2): 213–232.

McCann, L., Wankhade, P., and Murphy, P. (2019). Conclusion: Understanding emergency services in austerity conditions. In P. Wankhade, L. McCann, and P. Murphy (eds.), *Critical Perspectives on the Management and Organization of Emergency Services*. Abingdon: Routledge.

Moore-Bick, M. (2019). *Grenfell Tower Inquiry: Phase 1 Report*. London: TSO.

Murphy, P., Ferry, L., Glennon, R., and Greenhalgh, K. (2019). *Public Service Accountability: Rekindling a Debate*. Cham, Switzerland: Palgrave Macmillan.

Nelson, P.A., Cordingley, L., Kapur, N., Chew-Graham, C.A., Shaw, J., Smith, S., McGale, B., and McDonnell, S. (2020). 'We're the first port of call'—Perspectives of ambulance staff on responding to deaths by suicide: A qualitative study. *Frontiers in Psychology*. https://doi.org/10.3389/fpsyg.2020.00722

O'Flynn, J. (2007). From new public management to public value: Paradigmatic change and managerial implication. *Australian Journal of Public Administration*, 66(3): 353–366.

Pollitt, C., and Bouckaert, G. (2017). *Public Management Reform: A Comparative Analysis—Into the Age of Austerity*. Oxford: Oxford University Press.

Prosser, T., and Taylor, M. (2020). *The Grenfell Tower Fire: Benign Neglect and the Road to an Avoidable Tragedy*. Shoreham-by-Sea: Pavilion.

Santarone, K., McKenny, M., and Elkbuli, A. (2020). Preserving mental health and resilience in frontline healthcare workers during COVID-19. *American Journal of Emergency Medicine*, 38(7): 1530–1531.

US Government Printing Office. (2006). *Hurricane Katrina: A Nation Still Unprepared: Special Report of the Committee on Homeland Security and Governmental Affairs*. United States Senate. 109th Congress. 2nd Session, Special Report. S. Rept. 109–322. Available at: www.govinfo.gov/content/pkg/CRPT-109srpt322/pdf/CRPT-109srpt322.pdf

Wankhade, P. (2021). A 'journey of personal and professional emotions': Emergency ambulance professionals during COVID-19. *Public Money & Management*.

Wankhade, P., Heath, G., and Radcliffe, J. (2018). Cultural change and perpetuation in organisations: Evidence from an English emergency ambulance service. *Public Management Review*, 20(6): 923–948.

Wankhade, P., McCann, L., and Murphy, P. (eds.). (2019). *Critical Perspectives on the Management and Organization of Emergency Services*. New York: Routledge.

Wankhade, P., and Murphy, P. (2012). Bridging the theory and practice gap in emergency services research: Case for a new journal. *International Journal of Emergency Services*, 1(1): 4–9.

Wankhade, P., and Patnaik, S. (2019). *Collaboration and Governance in the Emergency Services: Issues, Opportunities and Challenges*. Cham, Switzerland: Palgrave Macmillan.

Wankhade, P., Stokes, P., Tarba, S., and Rodgers, P. (2020). Work intensification and ambidexterity—the notions of extreme and 'everyday' experiences in emergency contexts: Surfacing dynamics in the ambulance service. *Public Management Review*, 22(1): 48–74.

Wild, J., Greenberg, N., Moulds, M.L., Sharp, M.-L., Fear, N., Harvey, S., Wessely, S., and Bryant, R.A. (2020). Pre-incident training to build resilience in first-responders: Recommendations on what to and what not to do. *Psychiatry*, 83(2): 128–142.

Yates, J. (1999). Leadership in emergency services. *Australian Journal of Emergency Management*, 129(1): 62–65.

Zaré, M., and Afrouz, S. (2012). Crisis management of Tohoku; Japan Earthquake and Tsunami, 11 March 2011. *Iranian Journal of Public Health*, 41(6): 12–20.

Index

Printed in the United States
by Baker & Taylor Publisher Services